Feb-7-01

love belongs to those who do the feeling

Carol —

Hope you enjoy these
poems recent & from
long ago —
all the best —
love
Judy

love belongs to those who do the feeling

New & Selected Poems (1966–2006)

Judy Grahn

▼

RED HEN PRESS | LOS ANGELES, CALIFORNIA

love belongs to those who do the feeling

Book design by Mark E. Cull
Book layout by Jeff Takaki

ISBN: 978-1-59709-121-3
Library of Congress Catalog Card Number: 2008926154

The California Arts Council and the National Endowment for the Arts partially support Red Hen Press.

Red Hen Press
www.redhen.org

First Edition

Acknowledgements

First, to spirit, who does it all, my gratitude and awe.

Many thanks to this vivacious West Coast publisher, Red Hen Press, and Kate Gale, Terry Wolverton, Mark Cull, and all the staff.

Thoughtful critics help remind poets what we have set out to do and give us a sense of being reflected and held. I appreciate the written critiques and contextualization on my work by Adrienne Rich, the late Steve Abbott, Lynda Koolish, Sue-ellen Case, Mary J. Carruthers, Alicia Ostriker, Amitai F. Avi-ram, Margot Gayle Backus, Lynne Keller, Ron Silliman, Michael Davidson, Johanna Dehler, Linda Garber, Kim Whitehead, John Philip Chapin, Billie Maciunas, Delia Fisher, Ron Erickson, Joe W. Moffett, and anyone I don't yet know about.

For other kinds of support, I deeply appreciate profound partnerships with Yvonne Mary Robinson, Karla Tonella, Wendy Cadden, and Paula Gunn Allen; and all the members of the Women's Press Collective and Diana Press, of the Gay Women's Liberation households and of "A Woman's Place" Bookstore; and Kathryn Howd Machan; Rita Streicher, Marian Roth, Rachel DeVries; Blanche Wiesen Cook and Clare Coss; Diane DiPrima, Jack and Adelle Foley; the late Henry Noyes of China Books and Periodicals; the late Paul Mariah; Valerie Miner; the late Lee Frances; Elaine Gill and the late John Gill of The Crossing Press; Michael Denneny of St. Martin's Press; Joanne Wycoff and Deborah Chasman of Beacon Press; and from very long ago, Nathan Hare, Barbara Gittings, Larry Goodell; and the hundreds of patient people who organize readings and benefits, radio programs, theatrical events, and grassroots movements; and the myriad of people, including students such as Nisa Donnelly, Vanessa Tiegs, Anne Carol, Gregory Gajus and others, who have carried my poetic and philosophical work into the world in so many different forms. Thank you so much.

I am grateful for the (hopefully lifelong) ongoing deep or occasional heart conversations of collaboration that continue to nourish my life, spirit and mind, with my colleagues Betty De Shong Meador, Deborah Grenn, Laura K. Brown, Anne Bluethenthal, Luisah Teish, Vicki Noble, Charlene Spretnak, Neeli Cherkovski, Olympia Dukakis, Elinor Gadon, Lucia Birnbaum, Jean Weisinger, and over the distances with my comrades in art and change, Joy Harjo, Cherrie Moraga, Eloise Klein Healy, Minnie Bruce Pratt, Irena Klepfisz, the late Audre Lorde, the late Pat Parker, the late Gloria Anzaldua. As ever I praise the poetry of Sappho, Enheduanna and other poets of

Inanna, and Gertrude Stein, and turn now to joyfully engage with *The Devi Mahatmya*, Ilanko's *Tale of an Anklet*, *The Mahabharata* and some of the marvelous oral literature of India.

Finally, to my chosen family my love and thanks, thanks, thanks: to my beloved life partner, friend, and colleague Kris Brandenburger and my dear friends and colleagues Dianne E. Jenett and Edwin May, may we continue knowing each other for the sheer joy of it.

Contents

selections from
She Who (1972–1974)

selections from
Confrontations with the Devil in the Form of Love **(1975)**

selections from
The Queen of Wands (1980–1982)

selections from
The Queen of Swords (1986–1987)

New Poems (1987–2006)

love belongs to those who do the feeling

Introduction

CREATING A SOCIAL MOVEMENT

When Wendy Cadden and I arrived in 1968 the Bay Area was an intricate matrix of small presses and interlocking poetic voices, but gaining access was a different story. Looking for a door to anything, I joined a group sponsored by Society for Individual Rights, (SIR), a gay organization out of L.A. The poets who met were new gay voices, especially Paul Mariah, whose work was explicitly, sexually gay, and who, along with Richard Tagett began publishing *Manroot Magazine* in August of 1969; they published my work a number of times; Paul always reminded me he was the earliest publisher of my work aside from *Sexology Magazine* and *The Ladder*.

But Wendy and I were keenly pressured by the sexism throughout the Civil Rights movements in which we participated, and by November of 1969 historical forces swept me away from this sweet little poetry group, off into our own revolutionary movement—Gay Women's Liberation—which Wendy Cadden and five other women and I co-founded. It felt to us as though women had not talked to each other or defined our own issues ever, although similar conditions drove the First Wave of feminism, which culminated in women gaining the right to vote in 1919. Here we were fifty years later, in the middle of the great Civil Rights Movement, and experiencing deep disconnection as women and as lesbians. So, we established and ran women-owned institutions for public voice and action.

We immediately began publishing women-centered and lesbian-formulated work beginning with my own article "On the Development of a Purple Fist," and poetry, a mimeographed edition of *The Common Woman Poems*. We then continued editing other women's poetry, with Wendy Cadden editing the graphics for our unique anthology *Woman to Woman*. By 1970 we had used this work and my first collection of poetry, *Edward the Dyke and Other Poems*, which I ran off on a mimeograph machine, as the foundation of the Women's Press Collective, the second feminist press at the time.[1] By 1974 we had acquired and taught ourselves to run two printing presses, and published a number of germinally important poetry books and *Lesbians Speak Out*, a collectively edited anthology of lesbian feminist essays with beautiful illustrations.

I had first engaged with social change movements in the 1960;s and marched with Mattachine Society in a picket of the White House for Gay Rights in 1965, with Barbara Gittings, Frank Kameny and others. Gay Women's Liberation, feminism, a few working class Gay men, and various organizations of people of color kept the forward motion of social change going for another decade by forming our own movements in the late Sixties, sidestepping elements of the Left that were spiraling into anarchistic violence and militaristic confrontations with the state, just as the state was engaging in increasing violence in southeast Asia. From grassroots sources an explosion of poetry helped carry a new round of democratic messages to "the people." More specifically, the poetry helped create and define the goals of communities, and helped empower women especially, as well as disenfranchised men, to speak with their own voices and engage with the world. Those poems, including my own contributions, have been transformative of individual lives, and of social conditions.

DEVELOPING A POETIC VOICE

In the cauldron of the early second wave of feminist movement, from the Fall of 1969 when I sat down to replicate or fabricate, rather, a women's group that could include me (and other working class women) I laid down the first set of poems, *The Common Woman Poems*, that would establish a "voice," not for me as a poet, but for people who had been invisible. The poems were portraits, "americanized sonnets" as I imagined them, and they were visual and accessible, filled with sensual and hopefully empathy-inducing information, and through them, "ordinary" women jumped into historic and present time, acquiring an authentic presence and a reflection they seemed not to have experienced previously, to which legions of women responded. It was my intention for the poetry to

---

[1] The poet Alta, who published the magazine *Aldebaran Review* with her then-husband, the poet John Oliver Simon, established the first feminist press, Shameless Hussy.

16

institute a ceremonial quality to being female, a presence, a dignity and an authority that included "reality" and also drew on powers of nature and myth.

My earliest poetic voice—forged in communities of lesbian feminists, activist feminists, and disenfranchised gay men—featured sexual explicitness, previously unspeakable facts of women's and gay lives, emphatic oral rhythms, and what, especially in my nine part poem "A Woman Is Talking to Death" (1973) Kim Whitehead has called a "coalitional voice" that combines personal with collective and historic experience, to reach out to make alliances with other communities. The poems introduced terms that hadn't been featured in poetry: dyke, queen, queer, butch, bitch, whore, "She Who"—these and other phrases entered the language of acceptability and expectation: "bond between women," "women-loving-women" and always, "the common woman."

Being woman-centered and balancing metaphors with what I hoped were blazing critiques of power structures, this poetry has also been unexpectedly popular, indeed it is mostly ordinary people who keep it circulating. Despite a literary establishment suspicious of work that is too popular, it has been accepted as poetry. Yet in the standard literary and academic bastions, this poetry, so dear to the hearts and lives of many working class women and men, has been invisible. The irony should not escape us, since it reflects the state of the country as a whole. Haven't so many voices been stilled? Perhaps the poetry asks provocative questions. Can "woman" stand for human? Or must we all become men? Does God have any daughters, or peers? Does Walt Whitman? Do working class and poor people have minds, and rich histories, and great capacity to engage in civic life? Or are we just objects of sympathy? Is "dyke" to be a forbidden word even when deconstructed by a dyke? Or is transgender, as I believe, the beginning of a vast evolutionary step? And most important of all, are women fully active in directing this human adventure and empowered to take responsibility for all our impacts on this planet.

THREE RHYTHMS OF POWER

Between 1969 and 1972 I laid down some basic rhythms and intentions in two sets of poems, "The Common Woman Poems," (1969); and "She Who," (written in 1972 except the "Funeral Plainsong" written in 1974); and one nine-part poem, "A Woman Is Talking to Death," (1973). These three works would contribute to keeping a lot of social movement thrumming and spinning for a few decades. I delivered these poems orally on stage and in other venues hundreds of times. I read "She Who" for five years before we managed to publish it, so even without the work being printed, the poems spread through populations viscerally, like music.

The three sets each have what I imagine is a unique poetic voice: the sonnet-form visual portraits of seven different yet connected women in *The Common Woman Poems*, the grammatically fluid chants of *SheWho*, and the long-lined weave of intensely dramatic, even confrontational, narrative in *A Woman Is Talking to Death* established new patterns of form and content. These have continued to serve as wellsprings for my later work and also perhaps served as models for a substantial portion of the flood of gay/lesbian, feminist, women's, leftist and working class poetry that followed. In conjunction with the warrior sisters of my movement, especially poets Pat Parker and Willyce Kim, our readings were fiery, fierce, funny—whatever worked, right?, as we made every effort to drive the daring messages into the air like arrows.

SOME WAYS OF KNOWING THIS IS A "JUDY GRAHN POEM":

1. It's likely to be woman-centered or genderbending, and tries to be mindbending as well, so sometimes, it queers.
2. A poem is a container for love, so it's written for you—no matter who you are.
3. The intention is for both critique and solution, so my hope is that reading it can be transformative and experiential—a ritual.
4. The focus is serious and also very often humorous and whimsical, because if we can't laugh at ourselves how can we be spiritual?
5. It's not alienated even when it's angry: optimism furthers . . .
6. The poetry is "of use" to people in far flung circumstances, completely out of range of my personal or generational influence.
7. It has craft and musical sensibility, meant both to stand well on the page and to be satisfying to read out loud or perform.

COMMONALITY AND COMMUNITY

I am so tied to community for my writing, that if I don't have one I will go create one, just to have a community to write into; to connect with; to write from. To some extent this has been the primary way I have gotten my work to be understood; then community people of all descriptions carry it into the world, write it on walls, take it into classrooms, put it to music, put it up on their WEB sites, and simply refuse to let it disappear. The people who love it put it to "use."

That may seem strange to still need this conduit given that "accessible" is the number one description for my poetry, but I am not talking about style or form— I am talking about content. The content of my work has always been controversial, especially for folks who just don't want to engage with the necessity for social change. But what is love about if not looking after others?

Commonality holds individuality and difference within a context of possible unity. Commonality holds that we are at the center of some groups and the margins of others; overlapping boundaries of affinity and mutuality help us form alliances; our differences create a tension that stretches, teaches, and demands continual negotiation and occasional revolution.

Commonality is the overlapping of circles; there is not just one single circle with margins and center. While there are circles with fewer of certain kinds of resources and access, there are also "wealthy" circles that are "poor" and bereft of community or time or social values; there are "unwealthy" groups that have artful, dignified lives, and so on. Commonality asks people to look for what we have in common, and to respect and acknowledge differences. Commonality makes of every person a subject, not an object. Ideas and practices of commonality are not about trying to find one thing which we all must hold in common, like a common dream, or a common language, or a common set of ideal behaviors. Alliances are about different kinds of practical commonality, commonality of experience, need, purpose, intention, or direction: common cause. And within the multiple circles of commonality, common differences are not only allowed, they are expected, including differences in dreams, desires, and language; in economies, histories, psychologies, and spiritualities.

The portraits in *The Common Woman Poems* needed complicated metaphors to encompass life experiences that hadn't been made public, and were at that time shocking to people: responding with violence to the abuse of one's child; having an abortion; being secretly lesbian and self-sufficient; expressing brazen craziness and religious mysticism; coping with a mate's hatred of fatness; having to raise too many children, including those of the neighbors; being boss but not knowing how to hold authority. These subjects seemed overwhelming "unpoetic" and unspeakable in late 1968. I embedded the women in the truths of their life experiences with some common tools they use to get through the day (a flask/ escape, high heels/flirtation, apron/service, hammer and nails/independent competence, exotic hat/self expression, bread/communion) and then matched these with powers of nature: crow, snake, smoke, thunderstorm, sea water, monkey, third eye. Color seemed particularly necessary to give the portraits depth, so Detroit Annie's hat has outrageous black feathers, she is wine red as a metaphor of her real subjects, blood and capacity to dance right off the cliff.

The common women were composites, except for Vera, my mother. Detroit Annie (not her name) was modeled for several friends and also for an exceptionally intense person who sat in my lap (she was hitchhiking) on her way to Detroit. Within a few days we heard that she had immolated herself with gasoline in protest of the Vietnam War. I often think of her burning her own image into the sky over that terrible war, which like its match in Iraq, we could not bear, and did everything we could to stop our government from doing.

MYTHIC REALISM

Reading Kim Whitehead's *The Feminist Poetry Movement*, I was reminded of a term I have used to describe my work. "Mythic realism" is a description for what I do in poetry; descriing the cyclic shape of interaction between story and ritual (action). Myths derive from our lives; and we live them. As children we learn the myths expected of us, and the actions that go with them. We live lives that are guided by the myths of former generations and also by the specific circumstances of our own generation's "reality." As we live, we revise our actions to suit new circumstances. As we revise them, the mythmakers, poets,

20

philosophers, songwriters and filmmakers of our generation take note and write more appropriate versions of the myths.

Mythic realism seeks to challenge universal or static and disempowering myths of Western culture by using and transforming them into vital energized stories as possibilities for both women in particular and people in general. The tactic is one of shattering the original myth to produce new variants. I then attempt to hold these variations within a ritual drama that reveals facets. Realism, in the sense of contemporary and historic stories, (including pieces of my personal story) can thus engage the primal myth-stuff, merge with it and give it renewed life, emotion and meaning. The myth of Helen of Troy is particularly compelling because she already has so many facets, and was born of an egg, in a version in which her mother is Leda, a swan. The Troy story refers to a major war of Greeks against Trojans; they were fighting over the autonomy of Helen, who had left her Greek husband for a Trojan lover named Paris. I began my extensive journey with her in *The Queen of Wands* (1982) and continued in *The Queen of Swords*, 1987) casting her further back in time as Inanna, the Mesopotamian Venus of four to five thousand years ago. This second book- length poem utilizes the plot of recently translated Mesopotamian poetry, infusing ancient yet eerily familiar myths into my version. I modernized Helen in *Swords* by setting the scene in an underworld lesbian bar of contemporary times and letting a bunch of rather raucous characters, including the Amazon Warrior Penthesilea, who fought for her at Troy, put the modern Helen through a major transformation.

In a sense I have taken the literary idea "Helen" (as the beauty of all women) and splattered her as if she were an egg, except each splatter has a regenerative quality; they are not identical but they have the same substance. Beads of mercury do this when dropped; the central ball breaks into dozens of other balls, each having the same qualities of the original, and made of the same substance; and if you split each one again, they would again form smaller droplets with the same qualities as the original. *That* is the Helen I am imagining, not a single archetype— but instead a multicharacter, infinitely immanent, who crosses time and space, who lives simultaneously in "all of us."

I am writing four full length epic poems in this series. Two have been published. In *The Queen of Swords*, Helen is also shattered, this time of her own volition and psychologically as well as across time and space, and comes together as a new, far more complex kind of woman. By shattering the central figure of Helen into a dozen or a zillion "Helens," who have her qualities, so that her qualities are immanent within them, she becomes pervasive, like shakti, a life force, an intelligence of fire. As when a volcanic fire shatters into hundreds of fires. Helen has been so reduced in the story that has descended through Homer that filmmakers cast her as thin, blonde, young, sexually attractive and rather vacuous. The Helen in *Wands* has agency, and multiple human voices and also the voice of a creation spider, of a joyfully sexual tree, and of an "egg of being" that deliberately breaks itself open. When poet and Ithaca College professor Kathryn Howd Machan cast her version of *The Queen of Wands* for stage she used four Helens, each markedly different yet all having qualities of dignity, authority, authenticity, high drama, and beauty.

The third and fourth epics in this series are in process. I have included one poem, "To the Mother of All Bowls" in this collection, that will be part of The Queen of Cups, which features a meeting of Helen with Mother Goddesses of India set partly in the time of Jesus and partly in the present.

ONWARD AND ONWARD

For twenty three years I was able to operate as a freelance writer, and produce a body of work, then by the mid 1990's I lost all publishers, mostly because of quirks in the industry. Then, as postmodernism swept across the country and a backlash against anything associated with feminism took virulent form, the subject of lesbianism became mainstream and commercialized; women were trying on the new shoes feminists had made for them. Reluctantly I went back to school, hoping I could find ways to continue my work.

My life took a different course as I returned to school, earning a Ph.D. in Integral Studies, doing doctoral research on women's rituals in South India. As always my focus is on philosophical importance of the lives and accomplishments of those who do common work. I engage the academy with skepticism, wanting to be nonaffiliated; however in teaching I have found genuine community with beloved colleagues, and students. And that this poetry does not end, and neither do the movements from which it grows even as it feeds.

Every decade, it seems, a different Common Woman Poem is the popular one.

In 1971 or so, a multi-racial band, "High Risk," put jazz behind "Nadine resting on her neighbor's stoop," and Max Dashu made a gorgeous cover of the 45 recording with dramatic Amazons on horseback. Prior to this the final lines from "Vera, from my childhood" swept orally and then in grassroots poster versions across the country and by 1978 were showing up in the speeches of top democratic political women: "the common woman is as common as the best of bread/and will rise. . ." These and other common woman lines began showing up as graffiti in all kinds of places. Later they spread into the world, and a performance artist in Australia toured with them; lesbian feminists in Argentina read them in the Plaza de Las Madres, marching with a poster with my picture on it.

Later on through the late 1980's and 1990's, literature textbooks began reprinting "Ella, in a square apron, along Highway 80." Anthologies continued to include a wide range of my poems. But by the mid 1990's I thought the poems might have run their course despite my efforts to make them timeless. Then I looked on the WEB and there they were, people were refusing to let them disappear. They were putting them on their blogs. Modern American Poetry site had gone up, and there I was, written up by Mary J. Carruthers, Amitai F. Avi-ram, Michael Davidson, and others. A chorale group calling itself "She Who" issued a CD. In 2004 here was singer-songwriter Ani Di Franco reading "Detroit Annie, hitchhiking" at Carnegie Hall. A year later the poem was chosen to be embossed on a sidewalk in Berkeley as part of a poetry art project. As in the earlier generation, people continue to name their organizations (battered women's shelters, for instance) "Common Woman" after the poems, in the U.S. and in Canada. Earlier examples were a newspaper in Berkeley, a magazine (*Common Lives / Lesbian Lives*) in Iowa; a bookstore in Austin, a women's chorus in North Carolina, and so on. Variations of the general idea spread among the poets, such as "The Dream of a Common Language," "common desires," and "common differences," and (in reverse) "Uncommon Women."

Lately I see references to the lesbian portrait, "Carol, in the park, chewing on straws," on blogs. I also see quotes without credit, not because people are stealing but because they acquired the quote as it initially spread, anonymously, by word of mouth, all across the wide country. Despite all the readings I was doing, many people literally did not know who had written it, and in the days before women had access to presses, or bookstores promoting women's work, they had no way to find out. It has been important to me to make sure people know that a woman, *a working class lesbian woman*, had written the poems, so I have tried to chase it all down. Maybe you would help with that, if the occasion arises. Especially when church groups use any version of the "common woman is the best of bread and will rise" quote without knowing who wrote the words: I love it that people find these words inspiring, and I don't want any hypocrisy here, I want people to know: a very loving lesbian wrote those words, folks: *and*, she wrote them for her mom, who was a devout (mostly) Christian.

The inability of very many critics of the poetry establishment to take on my work as a whole (yet) is probably because of splits within the whole society—the early work establishing lesbian and women's community is grounded in reality, not the least bit "transcendental" or disembodied. The work establishing gay identity as more than behavior, as having intrinsic social and cultural "worth" was embraced by a generation of gay, lesbian and transgendered people, but its premise of them as change agents doesn't easily fit with the assimilationist drive of gay and lesbian families, and of those (perhaps not so many) transgendered people whose primary desire is to "fit in." Then too, what is "spirituality" to lefty liberal folks? And what is highly specialized "queer theory" to its own roots and to real life? Meantime, the women's spirituality movement is not sure what to do with lesbian imagery—you get the point. Like my late co-poet friend Pat Parker, (and not forgetting the white skin privilege I have that she did not) I too work for a world in which I can arrive with all my selves. But that painful and exhilarated weaving of fragmented aspects of society through one's own tender person is also the poet's task.

For me and for many in my generation, life is a calling, a focused drive. While I list the goals in a linear fashion, in reality they are completely interwoven:

the first task has been to make public voice with, for, and about women, and to surface with the realities of our lives. We have accomplished that to some extent. And now we need to get women into mass leadership positions along with equality-based men, and place women's concerns front and center for the country, and the world—that is to say, earth.

The second task has been to seize the means of reproduction and sexuality, taking control of our own bodies and our own sexual and relational desires and needs, our own definitions of family and community. This remains contested territory, though several international movements continue to spread and organize.

The third task has been to address the injustices of race and class in addition to gender; we have made some gains, some ghastly setbacks, we still have much to teach each other, and this remains a lifelong commitment to find methods of positive change that are effective.

The fourth task is to unearth women's hidden histories, mythologies, and spiritualities; and then do major revisions of who women have been, are and could be in the directing and creating of all aspects of culture. This work is beginning to surface in earnest. When I say "woman" I mean "womankind" in the sense of "women and their kindred"—as differentiated from the exclusionary patriarchal systems we intend to change.

These tasks, or missions, are implied in the "oath" of commonality and community, of solidarity and continued effort that appears in a number of places in the poetry. I remain tied to these oaths; they bond me to my lifework. I am allied with people who have made similar commitments to lead meaningful lives.

Dedication

To the Mother of All Bowls (2004)
for Luisah Teish

some bowls are cool
to the touch
some bowls are full of stew
some bowls don't hold
too much
what kind of bowl are you

though made of porcelain
some bowls last tens of centuries
though made of solid gold some bowls
change in a flash meltdown

some bowls age in penitentiaries
some begging bowls sit out on the ground
some bowls sing . . .
some bowls get passed around
for everyone to drink

some bowls get smashed
in the kitchen sink
some bowls stand still in the old bowl museum
some bowls go to every pot luck

some bowls overflow
some bowls suck it up
some bowls clutch ash in the mausoleum
some bowls hold hospital suffering

circling bowls alleviate
envy
water bowls consecrate
nativity
burning bowls emulate
eternity
flower bowls re-create
proclivity
red garuthi bowls
soak up soak up soak up
negativity

some bowls spill out in offering
some bowls transform
some bowls bring about a sea storm

some bowls say bowls
witness everything

She loves all bowls
She makes

all bowls break
all bowls return to Her

the Mother of all bowls

dishes up love,
that's why the love is
unconditional
unconditional love
belongs to bowls.

selections from

Edward the Dyke and Other Poems

(1966–1970)

I arrived in the Bay Area in 1968, having had a successful public reading in Albuquerque the year before, while living with Karla Tonella. She was so supportive of my early poetry that she rented a house in Placitas owned by the poet Robert Creeley, and moved us in there. I never met him, he was already in Buffalo, but I had been reading his poetry for years, and still can feel what an amazingly alchemical experience it was to sit in the tiny darkwood studio he had added to the adobe house, and work on myself as a poet. To have a little studio for writing! That was a new way of life for me; I used the studio during the day since I worked nights at the Albuquerque Indian Hospital.

But though the Black Mountain poets had the sparse directness I so appreciated for its promise of honesty, the poetry that swept over me in San Francisco to record workingclass and female experience bubbled up right out of the old English metaphoric style I had studied as a child, though forged in American directness and salted with my own Chicago-born version of terse: I'm not a girl/ I'm a hatchet/" and my New Mexico-raised version of nature: "I'm not a hole/ I'm a whole mountain."

The tenderness of love lost is in these poems "if you lose your lover/ rain hurt you. blackbirds/ brood over the sky trees/ burn down everywhere brown/ rabbits run under/ car wheels . . ." But you can also spot the political rage and desire for change that is welling up and finding its way to the river of social movement: "Suppose you have an elephant/ with 56 millimeter trunk/ . . . and drunk/ . . . and crazy . . . / How're you going to bring that elephant down?"

Now that remains a good question.

I'm not a girl

I'm not a girl
I'm a hatchet
I'm not a hole
I'm a whole mountain
I'm not a fool
I'm a survivor
I'm not a pearl
I'm the Atlantic Ocean
I'm not a good lay
I'm a straight razor
look at me as if you had never seen a woman before
I have red, red hands and much bitterness

Asking for Ruthie

you know her hustle
you know her white legs
flicker among headlights
and her eyes pick up the wind
while the fast hassle of living
ticks off her days
you know her ways

you know her hustle
you know her lonely pockets
lined with tricks
turned and forgotten
the men like mice hide
under her mind
lumpy, bigeyed
you know her pride

you know her blonde arms cut
by broken nickels in
hotelrooms and by razors of
summer lightning on the road
but you know the wizard
highway, no resisting so
she moves, she is forever missing

get her a stopping place
before the night slides dirty
fingers under her eyelids and
the weight of much bad kissing
breaks that ricepaper face

sun cover her, earth
make love to Ruthie
stake her to hot lunches in the wheat fields
make bunches of purple ravens
fly out in formation, over her eyes
and let her newest lovers
be gentle as women
and longer lasting.

the harvest spider

flowers on my wall

ornately

legs stretched long and

easy as a young queen

in the park

he knows his trick

will come and meanwhile

he's not asking

the centipede's poem

I never asked the reason
some are yellow owls
and some howl
I never asked an accounting of legs
or heart chambers
we walked out of the sea
on whatever we had to walk on
and some stayed in
there is every kind of animal
that there is
and neither the moon nor the man nor
the mango tree
answers it
I never asked why mice in a woodpile
were not me
I eat whatever I
eat go where I go and
sit quite still
breathing

in the place where

in the place where
her breasts come together
two thumbs' width of
channel ride my
eyes to anchor
hands to angle
in the place where
her legs come together
I said 'you smell like the
ocean' and lay down my tongue
beside the dark tooth edge
of sleeping
'swim' she told me and I
did, I did

If you lose your lover

if you lose your lover
rain hurt you. blackbirds
brood over the sky trees
burn down everywhere brown
rabbits run under
car wheels. should your
body cry? to feel such
blue and empty bed dont
bother. if you lose your
lover comb hair go here
or there get   another

The Marilyn Monroe Poem

I have come to claim
Marilyn Monroe's body
for the sake of my own.
dig it up, hand it over,
cram it in this paper sack.
hubba. hubba. hubba.
look at those luscious
long brown bones, that wide and crusty
pelvis. ha HA, oh she wanted so much to be serious

but she never stops smiling now.
Has she lost her mind?

Marilyn, be serious—they're taking
your picture, and they're taking the pictures
of eight young women in New York City
who murdered themselves for being pretty
by the same method as you, the very
next day, after you!
I have claimed their bodies too,
they smile up out of my paper sack
like brainless cinderellas.

the reporters are furious, they're asking
me questions
what right does a woman have
to Marilyn Monroe's body? and what
am I doing for lunch? They think I
mean to eat you. Their teeth are lurid

and they want to pose me, leaning
on the shovel, nude. Don't squint.

But when one of the reporters comes too close
I beat him, bust his camera
with your long, smooth thigh
and with your lovely knucklebone
I break his eye.

Long ago you wanted to write poems;
Be serious, Marilyn
I am going to take you in this paper sack
around the world, and
write on it:——the poems of Marilyn Monroe——
Dedicated to all princes,
the male poets who were so sorry to see you go,
before they had a crack at you.
They wept for you, and also
they wanted to stuff you
while you still had a little meat left
in useful places;
but they were too slow.

Now I shall take them my paper sack
and we shall act out a poem together:
"How would you like to see Marilyn Monroe,
in action, smiling, and without her clothes?"
We shall wait long enough to see them make familiar faces
and then I shall beat them with your skull.

hubba. hubba. hubba. hubba. hubba.
Marilyn, be serious
Today I have come to claim your body for my own.

Elephant Poem

Suppose you have an elephant
with 56 millimeter trunk
and say he's
                    tearing up the jungle
(say you think he's drunk
or crazy)
How're you going to bring that elephant down?
lion can't
bear could but don't want to
and the panther's too small for that job.

Then suppose you have an elephant
with million millimeter trunk
and his jungle is the whole green world?
(and drunk
and crazy)
you see the problem.
                    one more word
about elephants
No matter how hard they try
elephants cannot pick their noses
any more than bankers can hand out money
or police put away their pistols
or politicians get right with God.

a sty
in the elephant's eye
ain't nothing
but a fly in his nose
is a serious if not fatal condition

when the fly
gets into that nostril
it begins to swell
and stay closed
he can't smell can't drink can't think
can't get one up
on anybody
he begins to regret
all that flabby ammunition
hanging on him
he begins to wish
he'd been a little more bare-faced
like an ape or a fish
all those passageways
he needs to feed himself
tied up

ELEPHANT TURNED UPSIDE DOWN
by a fly
a million flies
outweigh a trunk
a tank
a bank
a million flies
outthink a pile of IBM
junk

we must be wise
to the elephant's lies

you may think we should try
to sober him up
but the trouble isn't that he's drunk
the trouble is
that he's an elephant
with multi-millimeter trunk
who believes the world is his jungle
and until he dies
he grows and grows

we must be flies
in the elephant's nose
ready to carry on
in every town
you know there are butterflies
there are horse flies and house flies
blue flies, shoo flies and it's-not-
true flies
then there are may flies and wood flies
but I'm talking about
can flies & do flies

glow flies, show flies, and make-it-so flies,
dragonflies and fireflies
in the elephant's nose
ready to carry on
til he goes down

A History of Lesbianism

How they came into the world
the women-loving-women
came in three by three
and four by four
the women-loving-women
came in ten by ten
and ten by ten again
until there were more
than you could count.

       they took care of each other
       the best they knew how
       and of each other's children,
       if they had any.

How they lived in the world,
the women-loving-women
learned as much as they were allowed
and walked and wore their clothes
the way they liked
whenever they could. They did whatever
they knew to be happy or free
and worked and worked and worked.
The women-loving-women
in America were called dykes
and some liked it
and some did not.

they made love to each other
the best they knew how
and for the best reasons

How they went out of the world,
the women-loving-women
went out one by one
having withstood greater and lesser
trials, and much hatred
from other people, they went out
one by one, each having tried
in her own way to overthrow
the rule of men over women,
they tried it one by one
and hundred by hundred,
until each came in her own way
to the end of her life
and died.

The subject of lesbianism
is very ordinary; it's the question
of male domination that makes everybody
angry.

the big horse woman

the big horse woman
walked out to the mountain
it was early in the morning
nobody was around

she was carrying a blanket
and she spread it on the ground
she sat down hard upon it
and made a moaning sound

the mountain wind was blowing
and she shuddered once or twice
as she pressed down on her belly
that was cold, and blue as ice

red was above the mountain
and red was in her eyes
and red the water running
on the big horse woman's thighs

a herd of speckled ponies
came up the hill behind
with four mares at the head
and two horse colts behind

and when she stood up finally
she smiled like a rising sun

and whatever she had on her mind
she didn't tell no one

this poem is called
how Naomi gets her period.

Vietnamese woman speaking
to an American soldier

Stack your body
on my body
make
      life
make children play
in my jungle hair
make rice flare into my sky like
whitest flak
the whitest flash
my eyes have
      burned out
looking
press your swelling weapon
here
between us   if you
push it quickly I should
   come
to understand your purpose
what you bring us
what you call it
there
in your country

The Common Woman Poems

(1969)

These poems were written in 1969, prior to our establishment of bookstores, presses, distribution and a "woman's market." The last seven lines of the seventh Common Woman poem, "Vera, from my childhood" were quoted and passed from person to person so thoroughly they became an anonymous talisman for the women's movement as a whole. At least three versions were reproduced on posters. One of these was accurate, but the others narrowed the meaning. Consider this one:

A common woman is
As common as a common loaf of bread—
AND WILL RISE.

Well, the quote is *sort of* correct, but off enough to drastically change and shortchange, the original meaning. Look at the original on pages 64–65 and you will immediately see what was lost in the oral passing from one woman to the next, across the country.

Though Vera is a specific person, "the common woman" can be any woman, but the bread is not just any bread. "the common woman is as common as the *best* of bread." The *best* of bread is the most carefully made, or the most sacred, is communion, or feeds everyone, or is the most nurturing substance we can imagine. "Common" steps outside of our factory driven lives to honor and treasure each of us, and in our commonality, to call for collectivity, alliance.

Then, the common woman doesn't only "rise," she also becomes "strong"— and that indicates political, economic and social power for an underclass that remains severely underrepresented. The US, for instance, is ranked 17th among industrial nations as good places to raise children.

For me, the oath of commitment has been an equally important part, renewed every time I read the poem in public: the "I swear it to you," swearing on one's own life, one's own head, to work indefinitely for the rise of women—whatever that might require. For the paraphraser, and much of the movement, evidently the rise of individual women one by one has been enough. For me there must be more. Today women have come a long way into the public sphere, and need to go much further; we need to be leading the country(ies), guiding them in some new directions, we need women's values, especially the values of mothers, guiding collective humanity, not simply "the rise" of individual women. And we must do this while holding families together, so this requires the caring participation and support of men—this is indeed a large oath, which is why it is emphasized in the poem.

I. Helen, at 9 am, at noon, at 5:15

Her ambition is to be more shiny
and metallic, black and purple as
a thief at midday; trying to make it
in a male form, she's become as
stiff as possible.
Wearing trim suits and spike heels,
she says "bust" instead of breast;
somewhere underneath she
misses love and trust, but she feels
that spite and malice are the
prices of success. She doesn't realize
yet, that she's missed success, also,
so her smile is sometimes still
genuine. After a while she'll be a real
killer, bitter and more wily, better at
pitting the men against each other
and getting the other women fired.
She constantly conspires.
Her grief expresses itself in fits of fury
over details, details take the place of meaning,
money takes the place of life.
She believes that people are lice
who eat her, so she bites first; her
thirst increases year by year and by the time
the sheen has disappeared from her black hair,
and tension makes her features unmistakably
ugly, she'll go mad. No one in particular
will care. As anyone who's had her for a boss

will know
the common woman is as common
as the common crow.

II. Ella, in a square apron, along Highway 80

She's a copperheaded waitress,
tired and sharp-worded, she hides
her bad brown tooth behind a wicked
smile, and flicks her ass
out of habit, to fend off the pass
that passes for affection.
She keeps her mind the way men
keep a knife—keen to strip the game
down to her size. She has a thin spine,
swallows her eggs cold, and tells lies.
She slaps a wet rag at the truck drivers
if they should complain. She understands
the necessity for pain, turns away
the smaller tips, out of pride, and
keeps a flask under the counter. Once,
she shot a lover who misused her child.
Before she got out of jail, the courts had pounced
and given the child away. Like some isolated lake,
her flat blue eyes take care of their own stark
bottoms. Her hands are nervous, curled, ready
to scrape.
The common woman is as common
as a rattlesnake.

III. Nadine, resting on her neighbor's stoop

She holds things together, collects bail,
makes the landlord patch the largest holes.
At the Sunday social she would spike
every drink, and offer you half of what she knows,
which is plenty. She pokes at the ruins of the city
like an armored tank; but she thinks
of herself as a ripsaw cutting through
knots in wood. Her sentences come out
like thick pine shanks
and her big hands fill the air like smoke.
She's a mud-chinked cabin in the slums,
sitting on the doorstep counting
rats and raising 15 children,
half of them her own. The neighborhood
would burn itself out without her;
one of these days she'll strike the spark herself.
She's made of grease
and metal, with a hard head
that makes the men around her seem frail.
The common woman is as common as
a nail.

IV. Carol, in the park, chewing on straws

She has taken a woman lover
whatever shall we do
she has taken a woman lover
how lucky it wasnt you
And all the day through she smiles and lies
and grits her teeth and pretends to be shy,
or weak, or busy. Then she goes home
and pounds her own nails, makes her own
bets, and fixes her own car, with her friend.
She goes as far
as women can go without protection
from men.
On weekends, she dreams of becoming a tree;
a tree that dreams it is ground up
and sent to the paper factory, where it
lies helpless in sheets, until it dreams
of becoming a paper airplane, and rises
on its own current; where it turns into a
bird, a great coasting bird that dreams of becoming
more free, even, than that—a feather, finally, or
a piece of air with lightning in it.

she has taken a woman lover
whatever can we say
She walks around all day
quietly, but underneath it
she's electric;
angry energy inside a passive form.
The common woman is as common
as a thunderstorm.

V. Detroit Annie, hitchhiking

Her words pour out as if her throat were a broken
artery and her mind were cut-glass, carelessly handled.
You imagine her in a huge velvet hat with great
dangling black feathers,
but she shaves her head instead
and goes for three-day midnight walks.
Sometimes she goes down to the dock and dances
off the end of it, simply to prove her belief
that people who cannot walk on water
are phonies, or dead.
When she is cruel, she is very, very
cool and when she is kind she is lavish.
Fishermen think perhaps she's a fish, but they're all
fools. She figured out that the only way
to keep from being frozen was to
stay in motion, and long ago converted
most of her flesh into liquid. Now when she
smells danger, she spills herself all over,
like gasoline, and lights it.
She leaves the taste of salt and iron
under your tongue, but you dont mind
The common woman is as common
as the reddest wine.

VI. Margaret, seen through a picture window

After she finished her first abortion
she stood for hours and watched it spinning in the
toilet, like a pale stool.
Some distortion of the rubber
doctors with their simple tubes and
complicated prices,
still makes her feel guilty.
White and yeasty.
All her broken bubbles push her down
into a shifting tide, where her own face
floats above her like the whole globe.
She lets her life go off and on
in a slow strobe.
At her last job she was fired for making
strikes, and talking out of turn;
now she stays home, a little blue around the edges.
Counting calories and staring at the empty
magazine pages, she hates her shape
and calls herself overweight.
Her husband calls her a big baboon.
Lusting for changes, she laughs through her
teeth, and wanders from room to room.
The common woman is as solemn as a monkey
or a new moon.

VII. Vera, from my childhood

Solemnly swearing, to swear as an oath to you
who have somehow gotten to be a pale old woman;
swearing, as if an oath could be wrapped around
your shoulders
like a new coat:
For your 28 dollars a week and the bastard boss
you never let yourself hate;
and the work, all the work you did at home
where you never got paid;
For your mouth that got thinner and thinner
until it disappeared as if you had choked on it,
watching the hard liquor break your fine husband down
into a dead joke.
For the strange mole, like a third eye
right in the middle of your forehead;
for your religion which insisted that people
are beautiful golden birds and must be preserved;
for your persistent nerve
and plain white talk—
the common woman is as common
as good bread
as common as when you couldnt go on
but did.
For all the world we didnt know we held in common
all along
the common woman is as common as the best of bread
and will rise

and will become strong—I swear it to you
I swear it to you on my own head
I swear it to you on my common
woman's
head

selections from

She Who

(1972–1974)

She Who is more vocal spiraling, than metaphorically structured, poetry. The stanzas are oral and sculptural, shaped by elemental rhythms, strongly motivated winds of whimsy, fury, and vital necessity, forming shapes noticed more deeply by the turning and twisting remaining after the willful breath of movement passes through.

"Goddess as a verb," as Alicia Ostriker has said. The related poems tell an origin story that begins now, with calling, not naming, that shakes into birth, that situates death in the cycles of life and its feedings; that cracks "dyke" from isolation into its familial components of daughter and grandmother; that locates the collective feminine at the place of continuance, of being, and of "first person."

To be the first person to oneself is to break the chains of servitude (though not of service). "Breast number one/ belongs to some, and/ breast number two/ belongs to you, and/ breast number three/ is She-Who-works-for-me." Twenty six years later I would read the poem in South India to an audience delighted to tell me that a goddess with three breasts lives in the nearby state of Tamil Nadu.

But no mystery here. California is saturated with Asian culture, and I had absorbed this image from a drawing by Betty Sutherland in *Woman to Woman* without effort or consciousness. Anyhow the grassroots Women's Spirituality Movement has been "breathing with" these poems since 1972, when they were written.

She Who

She Who
She, she SHE, she SHE, she WHO?
She – she WHO she – WHO she WHO – SHE?
She, she who? she WHO? she, WHO SHE?

who who SHE, she – who, she WHO – WHO?
She WHO – who, WHO – who, WHO – who, WHO – who . . .

She. who – WHO, she WHO. She WHO – who SHE?
who she SHE, who SHE she, SHE – who WHO—
She WHO?
She SHE who, She, she SHE
she SHE, she SHE who.
SHEEEE   WHOOOOO

She Who continues

She Who continues.
She Who has a being
named She Who is a being
named She Who carries her own name.
She Who turns things over.
She Who marks her own way, gathering.
She Who makes her own difference.
She Who differs, gathering her own events.
She Who gathers, gaining
She Who carries her own ways,
gathering She Who waits,
bearing She Who cares for her
own name, carrying She Who
bears, gathering She Who cares
for She Who gathers her own ways,
carrying
the names of She Who gather and gain,
singing: I am the woman, the woman
                  the woman – I am the first person.
and the first person is She Who is the first person to
She Who is the first person to no other. There is no
other first person.

She Who floods like a river and
like a river continues
She Who continues

parting on the left

parting on the left,
parting on the right,
braiding.

Sheep

The first four leaders had broken knees
The four old dams had broken knees
The flock would start to run, then freeze
The first four leaders had broken knees

'Why is the flock so docile?' asked the hawk.
'Yes, why *is* the flock so docile,' laughed the dog,

'The shepherd's mallet is in his hand,
The shepherd's hand is on the land,
The flock will start to run, then freeze—
The four old dams have broken knees,'
The dog explained.

The hawk exclaimed:
'The shepherd leads an easy life!'

'I know, I know,' cried the shepherd's wife,
'He dresses me out in a narrow skirt
and leaves me home to clean his dirt.
Whenever I try to run, I freeze—
All the old dams have broken knees.'

'Well, I'm so glad he doesn't dare
to bring his breaking power to bear
on *me*,' said the hawk, flying into the sun;
while the dog warned, in his dog run:
'Hawk—the shepherd has bought a gun!'

— — — — — — — —

'Why is the hawk so docile?' asked the flock,

'He fell to the ground in a feathery breeze;
He lies in a dumb lump under the trees.
We believe we'd rather have broken knees
Than lose our blood and suddenly freeze—
Like him.'

But the oldest dam gave her leg a lick,
And said, 'Some die slow and some die quick,
A few run away and the rest crawl,
But the shepherd never dies at all—
Damn his soul.

I'd will my wool to the shepherd's wife
If she could change the shepherd's life,
But I myself would bring him low
If only, *only* I knew how.'

She Who increases/what can be done

She Who increases
what can be done

I shall grow another breast
in the middle of my chest
what shall it be

not like the other ones lying there
those two fried eggs.

in the center of my flesh
I shall grow another breast
rounder than a ready fist,
slippery as a school of fish,
sounder than stone. Call it
She – Who – educates – my – chest.

She Who.

She is not my daughter, not my son
I'm going to groom her with my tongue
needle her senses with my pain
feed her hunches with my brain,

She Who defends me.

Breast number one
belongs to some, and
breast number two

belongs to you, and
breast number three
is She – Who – works – for – me

Now I have a longer tongue
and three good breasts, and some have none,
what can be done

The enemies of She Who call her various names

The enemies of She Who call her various names
a whore, a whore,
a fishwife a cunt a harlot a harlot a pussy
a doxie a tail a fishwife a whore a hole a slit
a cunt a bitch a slut a slit a hole a whore a hole
a vixen/a piece of ass/a dame — filly — mare
dove — cow — pig — chick — cat — kitten — bird
dog — dish/ a dumb blonde

you black bitch — you white bitch — you brown bitch — you
yellow bitch — you fat bitch — you stupid bitch — you stinking
bitch you little bitch — you old bitch — cheap bitch — a high
class bitch — a 2 bit whore — a 2 dollar whore — a ten dollar
whore — a million dollar mistress

    a hole a slut a cunt a slit a cut
    a slash a hole a slit a piece
    of shit, a piece of shit, a piece of shit

She who bears it

She who bears it
bear down, breathe
bear down, bear down, breathe
bear down, bear down, bear down, breathe

She Who lies down in the darkness and bears it
She Who lies down in the lightness and bears it
the labor of She Who carries and bears is the first labor

all over the world
the waters are breaking everywhere
everywhere the waters are breaking
the labor of She Who carries and bears
and raises and rears is the first labor,
there is no other first labor.

the many minnows

The many minnows are fishes that live in a stream,
and greedybeak is a bird that lives on the land
and comes down to the edge of the stream where he
sticks his head under the water and eats the
many minnows. After a long time of this greedybeak
had ate up all but 47 of the many minnows and they
were tired of it so the next time he approached
their stream they had a plan. They thrust all of their
silver scales and fins out as far as they would
go, and all in the same direction. The sun's rays
glinted off the silver scales and fins, and when
greedybeak looked down he saw nothing but his
own reflection. "There's another greedybeak down
there with MY fishes," he screamed and dove
straight into the water, in a rage. The 47
remaining many minnows promptly ate him up
and turned him into many more many minnows.

bowl of blood

She Who,
She Who carries herself in a bowl of blood
She Who holds a bowl of blood
and swallows a speck of foam
She Who molds her blood in a bowl
in a bowl, in a bowl of blood
and the bowl, and the bowl and the blood
and the foam and the bowl, and the bowl
and the blood belong to She Who holds it.

She shook it till it got some shape.
She shook it the first season and lost some teeth
She shook it the second season and lost some bone
She shook it the third season and some body was born,
She Who.

A Geology Lesson

Here, the sea strains to climb up on the land
and the wind blows dust in a single direction.
The trees bend themselves all one way
and volcanoes explode often.
Why is this?   Many years back
a woman of strong purpose
passed through this section
and everything else tried to follow.

The woman in three pieces

THE WOMAN IN THREE PIECES — ONE

She said she was unhappy and they said they would take care
of her. She said she needed love and so they raped her and
then she wanted to be alone. They locked her into a tiny
cell with one tiny window and took away her clothes,
turning off all the lights as they left. After a long while they
came back and she said, "It's so dark," so they shined a
very bright light into her face and she said "I don't like
that." "What's the matter" they said and she said "There
is nothing to eat, couldn't you please give me some water"
so they brought a hose and sprayed her hard with water.
"Are you happy now" they said and she answered "Please,
I'm so very cold, my bones ache and I shiver all the time."
So they brought huge piles of sticks and newspaper and built
a very large fire in her cell. She squeezed her body out of the
window and fell a great distance and was killed. "The trouble
with people like her" they said later "is that no matter how
hard you try to please them, they are never satisfied."

We said we were unhappy and they said they would take care of us. We needed love, they said, and so they raped us, and then they wanted to be alone. They locked us into a little cell with one tiny window and took away our clothes, turning off all the lights as they left. After a long while they came back and we said "It's so dark" so they shined a very bright light into our faces and we said "We don't really like that." "What's the matter" they said and we said "Well, there is nothing to eat, couldn't you please give us some water" so they brought a hose and sprayed us hard with water. "Are you happy now" they said and we answered "Please, we would be, but we're so very cold, our bones ache and we shiver all the time." So they brought huge piles of sticks and newspaper and built a very large fire in our cell. We squeezed our bodies out of the tiny window and fell a great distance and were killed. "The trouble with people like them" they said later among themselves, "is that no matter how hard they try to please us, we are never satisfied."

THE WOMAN IN THREE PIECES — THREE

I said I was unhappy and you said I would take care of him.
I needed love, he said, and so he raped you and then everyone
wanted to be alone.

We locked ourselves into a little cell with one tiny window
and took away our clothes, turning off all the lights as we
left.

After a long time we came back and I said "It's so dark" so
we shined a bright light into his face and you said "He
doesnt like that."

"What's the matter" I said and you said "There is nothing
to eat, couldnt you please give him some water?" So we
brought a hose and sprayed me hard with water.

"Are you happy now" I said and he answered, "Please, you
are so very cold, my bones ache and I shiver all the time."

So you brought huge piles of sticks and newspapers and he
built a very large fire in our cell.

You squeezed my body out of the window and we fell a
great distance and were killed.

"The trouble with people like us" we said later, "is that
no matter how hard I try to please you, I am never satisfied."

Carol and her crescent wrench

Carol and
her crescent wrench
work bench
wooden fence
wide stance
Carol and her
pipe wrench
pipe smoke
pipe line
high climb
smoke eyes
chicken wire
Carol and her
hack saw
well worn
torn back
bad spine
never – mind
timberline
clear mind
Carol and her
hard glance
stiff dance
clean pants
bad ass
lumberjack's
wood ax

Carol and her
big son
shot gun
lot done
not done
never bored
do more
do less
try to rest
Carol and her
new lands
small hands
big plans
Carol and her
long time
out shine
worm gear
warm beer
quick tears
dont stare
Carol is another
queer
chickadee
like me, but Carol does
everything
better
if you let her.

the most blonde woman in the world

The most blonde woman in the world
one day threw off her skin
her hair, threw off her hair, declaring
"Whosoever chooses to love me
chooses to love a bald woman
with bleeding pores."
Those who came then as her lovers
were small hard-bodied spiders
with dark eyes and an excellent
knowledge of weaving.
They spun her blood into long strands,
and altogether wove millions of red
webs, webs red in the afternoon sun.
"Now," she said, "Now I am expertly loved,
and now I am beautiful."

I am the wall at the lip of the water

I am the wall at the lip of the water
I am the rock that refused to be battered
I am the dyke in the matter, the other
I am the wall with the womanly swagger
I am the dragon, the dangerous dagger
I am the bulldyke, the bulldagger

and I have been many a wicked grandmother
and I shall be many a wicked daughter.

a funeral: plainsong from a younger woman to an older woman

i will be your mouth now, to do your singing
breath belongs to those who do the breathing.
warm life, as it passes through your fingers
flares up in the very hands you will be leaving

you have left, what is left
for the bond between women is a circle
we are together within it.

i am your best, i am your kind
kind of my kind, i am your wish
wish of my wish, i am your breast
breast of my breast, i am your mind
mind of my mind, i am your flesh
i am your kind, i am your wish
kind of my kind, i am your best

now you have left you can be
wherever the fire is when it blows itself out.
now you are a voice in any wind
      i am a single wind
now you are any source of a fire
      i am a single fire

wherever you go to, i will arrive
whatever i have been, you will come back to
wherever you leave off, i will inherit
whatever i resurrect, you shall have it

you have right, what is right
for the bond between women is returning
we are endlessly within it
and endlessly apart within it.
it is not finished
it will not be finished

i will be your heart now, to do your loving
love belongs to those who do the feeling.

life, as it stands so still along your fingers
beats in my hands, the hands i will, believing
that you have become she, who is not, any longer
somewhere in particular

we are together in your stillness
you have wished us a bonded life

love of my love, i am your breast
arm of my arm, i am your strength
breath of my breath, i am your foot
thigh of my thigh, back of my back
eye of my eye, beat of my beat
kind of my kind, i am your best

when you were dead i said you had gone to the mountain

the trees do not yet speak of you

a mountain when it is no longer
a mountain, goes to the sea
when the sea dies it goes to the rain
when the rain dies it goes to the grain
when the grain dies it goes to the flesh
when the flesh dies it goes to the mountain

now you have left, you can wander
will you tell whoever could listen
tell all the voices who speak to younger women
tell all the voices   who speak to us when we need it
that the love between women is a circle
and is not finished

wherever I go to, you will arrive
whatever you have been, i will come back to
wherever i leave off, you will inherit
whatever you resurrect, we shall have it
we shall have it, we have right

and you have left, what is left

i will take your part now, to do your daring
lots belong to those who do the sharing.
i will be your fight now, to do your winning
as the bond between women is beginning
in the middle at the end
my first beloved, present friend
if I could die like the next rain

i'd call you by your mountain name
and rain on you

want of my want, i am your lust
wave of my wave, i am your crest
earth of my earth, i am your crust
may of my may, i am your must
kind of my kind, i am your best

tallest mountain least mouse
least mountain tallest mouse

you have put your very breath upon mine
i shall wrap my entire fist around you
i can touch any woman's lip to remember

we are together in my motion
you have wished us a bonded life

*a funeral: for my first lover and longtime friend
Yvonne Mary Robinson b. Oct. 20, 1939; d. Nov. 1974
for ritual use only*

Slowly: a plainsong from an older woman to a younger woman

am I not   olden olden olden
it is unwanted.

wanting, wanting
am I not   broken
stolen   common

am I not crinkled cranky poison
am I not glinty-eyed and frozen

am I not   aged
shaky   glazing
am I not   hazy
guarded   craven

am I not   only
stingy   little
am I not   simple
brittle   spitting

was I not   over
over   ridden?

it is a long story
will you be proud to be my version?

it is unwritten.

writing, writing
am I not   ancient
raging   patient

am I not   able
charming   stable
was I not   building
forming   braving

was I not   ruling
guiding   naming
was I not   brazen
crazy   chosen

even the stones would do my bidding?

it is a long story
am I not proud to be your version?

it is unspoken.

speaking, speaking
am I not   elder
berry
brandy

are you not wine before you find me
in your own beaker?

do you not turn away your shoulder?
have I not shut my mouth against you?

are you not shamed to treat me meanly
when you discover you become me?
are you not proud that you become me?

I will not shut my mouth against you.
do you not turn away your shoulder.
we who brew in the same bitters
that boil us away
we both need stronger water.

we're touched by a similar nerve.

I am new like your daughter.
I am the will, and the riverbed
made bolder
by you – my oldest river –
you are the way.

are we not   olden, olden, olden.

Foam on the rim of the glass

Foam on the rim of the glass
another wave breaking

foam on the rim of the glass
another wave breaking
she once wanted to be a sailor

now she sits at the bar, drinking
like a sailor

the woman whose head is on fire

the woman whose head is on fire
the woman with a noisy voice
the woman with too many fingers
the woman who never smiled once in her life
the woman with a boney body
the woman with moles all over her

the woman who cut off her breast
the woman with a large bobbing head
the woman with one glass eye
the woman with broad shoulders
the woman with callused elbows
the woman with a sunken chest
the woman who is part giraffe

the woman with five gold teeth
the woman who looks straight ahead
the woman with enormous knees
the woman who can lick her own clitoris
the woman who screams on the trumpet
the woman whose toes grew together
the woman who says I am what I am

the woman with rice under her skin
the woman who owns a machete
the woman who plants potatoes
the woman who murders the kangaroo
the woman who stuffs clothing into a sack
the woman who makes a great racket

the woman who fixes machines
the women whose chin is sticking out
the woman who says I will be

the woman who carries laundry on her head
the woman who is part horse
the woman who asks so many questions
the woman who cut somebody's throat

the woman who gathers peaches
the woman who carries jars on her head
the woman who howls
the woman whose nose is broken
the woman who constructs buildings
the woman who has fits on the floor
the woman who makes rain happen
the woman who refuses to menstruate

the woman who sets broken bones
the women who sleeps out on the street
the woman who plays the drums
the woman who is part grasshopper
the woman who herds cattle
the woman whose will is unbending
the woman who hates kittens

the woman who escaped from the jailhouse
the woman who is walking across the desert
the woman who buries the dead

the woman who taught herself writing
the woman who skins rabbits
the woman who believes her own word
the woman who chews bearskin
the woman who eats cocaine
the woman who thinks about everything

the woman who has the tattoo of a bird
the woman who puts things together
the woman who squats on her haunches
the woman whose children are all different   colors

singing   i am the will of the woman
                 the woman
                 my will is unbending

when She-Who-moves-the-earth will turn over
when She Who moves, the earth will turn over.

selections from

Confrontations with the Devil in the Form of Love

(1975)

This oddly indefinable set of short poems falls between cracks, and I don't know what I think of them. Seldom do think of them. Then when they pop up on the WEB or other places I am surprised. They attempt to push a definition of love beyond the bitter illusions of fantasy and projection, and into substantive subjects, provision, power, commitment to great human effort, "my two hands."

Love isn't what doesn't come through for you or grinds you down with its rage or inability to see what is needed. Nor is it a rescuing device; "Love/ like anybody else, comes to those who/ wait actively/ and leave their windows open—"

Love shows up and does what is needed for a purposeful life.

The acidic tongue in cheek quality of some of these poems coupled with the sheer romanticism of others makes them fun to read because you can be sardonic one moment and completely vulnerable and sentimental the next: "Venus dear/ where *are* your arms?/ the trees have so many/ and no one thinks less of them for it" And then follow this with, "look at my lips/ they are apples/ my eyes are apples/ my life is an/ apple tree." The sensation I have reading them is like saying what you really want, then melting into a lover's arms by offering everything, and feeling that Love is a message of joy sent by life itself, flowing through us. Flowing, sometimes, through the poetry.

what do I have if not my 2 hands

what do I have if not my 2 hands
& my apples
Look at my lips
they are apples
my eyes are apples
my life is an
apple tree

Love came along   and saved me saved me

Love came along   and saved me saved me
Love came along and
after that I did not feel like fighting for
anything anymore after all
didnt I have   not that I had
anything to speak of
OR keep quiet about
but didnt I have
company in my nothing?
someone to say You're Great, to shout you are
wonderful, to whisper to me you are my every little thing?
& then one day Love left to go save someone else.
Love ran off with all my self esteem my sense of being
wonderful and all my nothing.
now I am in the hole.

you are what is female

you are what is female
you shall be called Eve.
and what is masculine shall be called God.

And from your name Eve we shall take
the word Evil.
and from God's, the word Good.
now you understand patriarchal morality.

Love is a space which is attracted

Love is a space which is attracted
to energy and repelled by
vacuums.
does that say anything to you
about what irritates me
when you speak only of what you have to need
and never what you need to have to offer?

Love came along and saved me

Love came along and saved me
        saved me   saved
me.
However, my life remains the same as before.
O What shall I do now that I *have*
what I've always been looking for.

Venus, ever since they knocked

Venus, ever since they knocked
your block off
your face is so vacant
waiting to be moved in on
by men's imaginations.
how could anybody love you?
having the ugliest mug in the world,
the one that's missing.

Love, you wicked dog

Love, you wicked dog
so handsome to look at,
so awkward close up
& so unfaithful to good sense.
Whoever feeds you attention
gets you, like it or not. And
all your bad habits come with
you like a pack of fleas.
Wherever I turn for peace of mind
there is the Love dog scratching
at the door of my lonesomeness,
beating her tail against the leg
of my heart
& panting all night with red breath
in my dreams.
Love dog! Get in or out
of the house of my life, stop chewing
on my belongings, the papers &
shoes of my independence.

Look at my hands

Look at my hands
they are apples
my breasts
are apples
my heart
is an apple tree

Love came along and saved

Love came along and saved
no one
Love came along, went broke
got busted, was run out of
town and desperately needs—
something. Don't tell her it's Love.

Venus, dear, where are your arms?

Venus, dear, where are your arms?
if only you were a tree.
they have so many,
& no one thinks less of them for it.

Ah Love, you smell of petroleum

Ah Love, you smell of petroleum
and overwork
with grease on your fingernails,
paint in your hair
there is a pained look in your eye
from no appreciation
you speak to me of the lilacs
and appleblossoms we ought to have
the banquets we should be serving,
afterwards rubbing each other for hours
with tenderness and genuine
olive oil
someday. Meantime here is your cracked plate
with spaghetti. Wash your hands &
touch me, praise
my cooking. I shall praise your calluses.
we shall dance in the kitchen
of our imagination.

Love rode 1500 miles on a grey

Love rode 1500 miles on a grey
hound bus & climbed in my window
one night to surprise
both of us.
the pleasure of that sleepy
shock has lasted a decade
now or more because she is
always still doing it and I am
always still pleased. I do indeed like
aggressive women
who come half a continent
just for me; I am not saying that patience
is virtuous, Love
like anybody else, comes to those who
wait actively
& leave their windows open.

This is what is so odd

This is what is so odd
about your death:
that you will be 34 years old
the rest of my life.
We always said that we would be around
we two,
in our old age
& I still believe that,
however when I am 80
you will still be 34,
& how can we ever understand
what each other has been through?

Young Love

Love's grandmother was a relatively
young woman, though completely blind
from diabetes. When Love was nine
she often took her to the doctor.
They lived alone together on Love's
petty thievery & whatever monthly
checks she rescued from the naked
mailbox. Love was already a fox
& her grandmother's sole support,
who had recently lost 4 toes to
gangrene, which would later take her foot
& then her leg. On this particular, eternal
day, the doctor went behind his screen
to write on a prescription pad
in careful, cryptic, doctor script,
a diet   anyone who was not him
could not afford. He was a real breadwinner.
He gave this list to Love, for her to put into accord.
& then he went to dinner.
Love never did decipher
his prescribed solution to their lives,
although she kept the piece of paper
in her one dress pocket
til it faded away
and worked to understand it every day
that winter.

Long after her grandmother had died
that summer, Love, until she grew up

& found out better,
believed that if only she had been able
to read the doctor's secret, scribbled letters,
her grandmother would have survived.
— & it was then she began to think
of revolution.

I only have one reason for living

I only have one reason for living
and that's you
And if I didn't have you as a
reason for living,
I would think of something else.

The poverty of love is when

The poverty of Love is when
the people are feeling hopeless
& their anger comes to live
like a bore worm in the apple of their eye.

After the boss took over:

After the boss took over:
Love had millions of babies
she didn't want—
and loved them anyway,
as the earth loves
even the fruits forced out of her
though she never forgives them.

Love said:

Love said:
look at my years
they are apples
my weeks are apples
my day
is an apple tree.

My name is Judith, meaning

My name is Judith, meaning
She Who Is Praised
I do not want to be called praised
I want to be called The Power of Love.

if Love means protect then whenever I do not
defend you
I cannot call my name Love.
if Love means rebirth then when I see us
dead on our feet
I cannot call my name Love.
if Love means provide & I cannot
provide for you
why would you call my name Love?

do not mistake my breasts
for mounds of potatoes
or my belly for a great roast duck.
do not take my lips for a streak of luck
nor my neck for an appletree,
do not believe my eyes are a warm swarm of bees;
do not get Love mixed up with me.

Don't misunderstand my hands
for a church with a steeple,
open the fingers & out come the people;
nor take my feet to be acres of solid brown earth,
or anything else of infinite worth

to you, my brawny turtledove;
do not get me mixed up with Love.

not until we have ground we call our own
to stand on
& weapons of our own in hand
& some kind of friends around us
will anyone ever call our name Love,
& then when we do we will all call ourselves
grand, muscley names:
the Protection of Love,
the Provision of Love & the
Power of Love.
until then, my sweethearts,
let us speak simply of
romance, which is so much
easier and so much less
than any of us deserve.

selections from

The Queen of Wands

(1980–1982)

My attention was drawn to the person of Helen when Bella Vivante (Zweig) offered a course on her as both goddess and queen. Reading Homer, Euripides, Sappho and H.D., I engaged with the archetypal character of Helen as "work" and also as "wisdom" since she is related to the Gnostic Feminine principle of Sophia.

I see all my mythic-based work as a continuation of my love for working class voices, (so I call it mythic realism) and with *The Queen of Wands* I am conscientiously criss-crossing time and space barriers to create a Helen who lives both in her history and also in the now, and is immanent in real people. So I have attempted to shatter the myth into a kaleidoscope of possible "Helens." Helen has been most often associated with upperclass and "white" standards of beauty, and with queenship, with being a goddess, with causing a great war; but her history is much more interesting than that; she is a woman who takes a fall, rises, takes a fall again; and who is sometimes at the height of power and glory and sometimes at the lowest end of the social scale—she is both goddess and slut, queen and slave, and in my version, she is also ordinary working women/people. Her "beauty" is so many values we can love or desire, including freedom; it is also the life energy that every worker contributes to the acts of living in a "factory" world.

This reminds us that any person or nation can be captured (or transfixed) in a tyranny whose grasp can be broken only through conscious concerted action.

"Who shall wake us if we don't ourselves?" "Mothers mothers raise him/ tell him, make him/ . . . who will wake us/ from our trance of ages/ if we don't ourselves . . ."

They say she is veiled

They say she is veiled
and a mystery. That is
one way of looking.
Another
is that she is where
she always has been, exactly in place,
and it is we,
we who are mystified,
we who are veiled
and without faces.

The land that I grew up on is a rock

I.

From my mother, a rock,
I have learned that rocks give
most of all.
What do rocks do? They hold the
forces of the earth together and
give direction. They interrupt
the mindless sky in its total
free fall.
Rocks turn the monotonous winds
from their courses and bring down rain
before the all-collecting sea
reclaims it—so you and your friends
can have some, too.
A rock is a slow, slow
cooled-off flame, and a cradle, both.

They are like bone, the rocks. They frame.
They remain. They hold you.
They grind together to make digestible dirt.
Because of their slow lasting
nature, they are said
not to feel tangible hurt.
We were star-struck, my father and I.
We ate fast intellectual pie.
And we made fun of her, my mother;
she made material, actual pie.

But once, in a flash of insight,
he said of my mother: "Without her,
people like you and I would fly
right off the earth."

He made a gesture of his hand helplessly
sucked into the sky (like a navigationless bird).
He knew she was a rock
and so did I. He knew the worth
of gravity and certain repetition,
the safety of enclosure.
I knew the mute, the flame-charred
female wall, the dam
of granite rock between one's child self
and the molten family core,
the hell of terror, the inner and the outer
fire: my father's ire.

II.

"You never listened to me."
Unexpectedly my mother weeps, recalling
how we never took her on our flights of thought
or left her, her own falling-out time.
How we locked her from our patch of
significant sky (that she was holding still for us)
my father and I,
as though she were a sheer wall of will

to be mined
to mill
and to grind and to be there
with or without our care.
It is so shocking for us
to see her now, a rock
weeping.

She is rocking
in her rocking chair
a little madly, deliberately deaf
to our star-struck talk.
She is chalk.

III.

This lasts only a moment, a few years,
for my mother's tears
quickly evaporate and
return to their own mother, the sky
who weeps intermittently over everything,
renewing
without care,
and with the greatest care,
especially over the rocks,
bathing and cooling them
who by their basalt nature
cradle their feelings for the

longest time and most profoundly,
taking continuous
though sometimes secret, pride
in what they give
and giving the most of all.

Whether we (sky divers) care to learn
how to share this treasure,
my mother's spirit will return and return
teaching us. Whether my father and I
will learn, or not.

"Your mother is a saint," he says.
He means,
the center of a rock, particularly
the one we live on,
is molten like a star, the core
is light,
enlightening, giving of
intelligence.
Stretched far into the cold unwieldy sky
my father and I
in reaching for a star,

we nearly overlooked the one
that pulsed, all that time,
there (beneath us)
under our floating feet , and *in* us,
in the person of my mother,

rocking sometimes somewhat madly
in her brilliance-giving vision,
as the earth,
a rock, a star.

A dream of Helen

The sun is a wild pumpkin this Fall.
The still lake surface is a mirror,
and I can see myself reflected:
I am the fairest of them all,
elderly, tall, bedecked with leaves,
my round brown branches are
flung wide as arms
and I am waiting.
My roots are woven to the bank
whereby I stand
to watch the Swans come down
like gods
to light upon the crystal lake,
to land like beams of light
upon the surface of an eye.

I wait. The air grows crisp.
My leaves curl and dry.
I watch the sky.
Everything is perfect and perfectly
connected, from the humming
of the insects to the footprints
of the bears, at the base
of my spine.
I am certainly perfect, in my
prime.
The air, everything is so still,

it is so clear that I will hold him
in my lake-reflected arms, the one who is
the first one down.

The great Swan. I will hold him
while he dances out his message
on my wide-flung limbs
in that split second
just before the image breaks,
just before the gossamer, the
netlike water, tears
to let him in.

What symmetry of quality
that memory has
of what a lovely world
that was.

2. THE EGG OF BEING SPEAKS:

My mother plucked me
from the great dance
of great birds
flying like stars, points
of light on maps
moving in the velvet wall
of night sky.
And I was called

the Daughter of Memory
and the Grandchild of Time.

My mother pushed me, wailing
from her yoni basket.
I lay on the wet green grass,
the perfect oval with a golden heart,
a world inside, a cluster
of amber possibilities, a
shell-cased spinner of flesh
and bone just waiting to be found,
to open, to be taken home.

My mother tied me
in her apron string, then
cut me from her cord
and let me go,
a perfectly knitted knot,
a wick.

My mother lit me
on her lap, an altar
and I was called the Flame
of Life, El-Ana,
gathering of forces
Beauty. Motion. Harmony.
Attraction.

My mother thought me
in one golden flash.
She had that kind of mind.
But I set out to do more
than think, to do the next
task, to break, to ask,
to fall all the way down,
to find, be found, to ken,
and to do more than stand.
To understand.

The meanings in the pattern

The interior of the Arizona Indian museum
is cool. A woman stands at the counter,
selling her family wares. "I am a Pima,"
she says. "We have always been here.
People say, where did the Anasazi go?
But we are right here, we never left.
We were farmers, always.
We were promised water for our gardens,
now they are taking it. My daughter
made the baskets; only girls are taught
to do it. My son made this pouch."
She pats the small soft leather purse,
thick with close beading, red and white,
yellow and blue. The design: clouds,
a bird, a man, the earth.
"This picture tells a story," she says.
Her black eyes looking inward and outward.
"No one who buys this could ever understand—
the meanings in the pattern. What it is
really worth." Clouds. A
bird. A man. The earth. Her fingers
feel the beads. "There is a story here.
It takes three days and nights to tell it."

Queen Helen

A queen am I
Queen Helen is my title.
As the sun shines so shines Helen
most beautiful.
I am what ever is
the weaving tree
and Mother of my people

I was Sovereign of my homespun folk
with their sheepshorn woolly garments.
We were considered most ascetic,
most athletic and democratic,
and I was entirely settled in my queendom
with my husband and my child,
when one day a young man came by
and I was undone.
He had won a contest
with the gods. I was the prize.
I was the golden apple
he had won. He, Paris, took me home
to his own land.

"Husband I am leaving,"
was my song.

> Husband I am leaving you,
> have left. And my homeland,
> child, and precious people;

all the wild, wild island
of my queendom.

I believe it was a matter of the
time, of Fate, a cosmic binding
and unbinding.
Ties I felt to go
pulled harder than the ties
I felt to stay.
Had my power been slipping?

Did you get the message I had
pinned for you to see:
"I want my full measure of reality,
I don't want the numb illusion.
Only sightfulness can make us see.
Only freedom makes us free."

Foolish words probably,
of a queen wrenched from her earth,
a queen taking to the air,
a queen flying.
Yet I feel a new fertility . . .

I moved my queendom and my court,
my ladies and my special looms I brought
with me as well as the hearthfire
that was my totem,

"Heart of the sky,"
and heart of the house
of Helena at Sparta.

"Lilanna," Queen of sheep-folds
they called me,
who causes the earth to quake.
Mother of the temple
and of the people,
Nana.
A Queen am I
Queen Helen and a Sovereign,
Flama. Shaker
alike of earth and of the heavens.

Without his heart he ranted
thinking it was me he wanted,
thinking that he could not live
or rule without me.
And the women I left knitting
at his palace
needled and poked incessantly,
until his pride bled

and his whole brain broke.
Who does Helen think she is, they said,
to go among strangers,
and to let herself be prized

so highly, to be called 'the fairest.'
Haughtiest of dames and proudest,
has she never heard of 'modest'?
Sitting in the Trojan tower,
does she think she has such power,
does she think she is a goddess?

Here is what I know:
Even the most golden
golden apple sometimes
rolls down the long wand limb
and lands in the lap of fire.

In ships he came to me,
in ships surrounded.
I was dumbfounded.
A thousand ships, so many!
where had he gotten them?
They filled the harbor
like a bobbing forest.
I was almost proud:
I stood on the ramparts of the city
and exclaimed out loud.

None of us knew the war would
last so long
and be so boring.
None of us knew we women were already

in prison. We sat in the weaving room
month on month, winding the distaff,
working the shuttle,
with only our own housebound prattle,
with never anything fresh, not air
or news or love or food.

We entertained each other
with bawdy jokes and stories
and a tapestry that told the progress
of the war. We comforted the new
widows. The bone-torn mothers.
Subject we were to every nervous stew of
scary rumors. No one danced.
Almost, we lost our glow. Ten
years passed. At least the men
had action—however many bodies paid for it.
And we all held fast, somehow.

In the tenth year it was clear
that those from the ships
had lost. They quarreled
and skulked and bled.
Stench of the burning dead
came to our noses even in
the weaving room.
And they had stopped singing at night
or calling out my name

in derision or admiration
or lust.

They had lost, their shoulders sagged.
They won battle after battle without
taking the city or getting near me.
We no longer lived in so much dread.
We waited for surrender to be said.
But they were unjust.

And they won it finally with a lie,
hypocrisy,
the offer of friendship
with soldiers in its belly.
They won it with
the lie, hidden under honey
like a razor in the bread.

        I too fell for the lovely painted horse,
        with his wide nose flaring.
        I too wished to have a party and be daring.
        Queen of morbid siege was I,
        Queen only by my title,
        and I too grabbed for the sudden win,
        the grinning, golden bridle.
        Forgotten were the lessons
        of want and pain,
        the bodies dragged round
        the walls of our emotion.

He was glinting like the sun
or like an apple. He was
neither; he was a bomb exploding
in the last battle.
Years of boredom
and regret blanked out as
I reached to embrace, to bind,
to pull him nearer with his
sparkling, blinding cargo.

We cheered when we had got him
all the way in. And then he flamed
into a torch and tortured;
seared the city down to ash and
rubble twenty centuries could
not even find.
And I began to live the recent
history of my kind.

All that night
we clung in tiny groups together
watching Paris and every
other Trojan man
die, too shocked to cry.
Thousands of corpses, so many!
such a limp crowd. I stood on
the ramparts of the tower and
exclaimed out loud.

So Helen fell like a pretty city
into the lap of war, a husband's war
against her.

A queen am I, Queen Helen
is my title.
Queen at the heart of the greatest
Western battle—
they have said was all on my account.

They have said the war was on my account,
my "beauty," they said, as though beauty
is something someone else can capture.
As though the Flame transfers.

I went out a Queen
a Sovereign, Mother of my people
and a lover—

I came back a captive.
My husband had gone out
a King, a Sovereign
and a soldier.
He came back a tyrant,
a master of slaves—
and I came back a slave.

For the first time
when he put his hands

upon me, I was afraid.
I was positively filled
with fear. He chased me
through my own halls,
even into my temple. I
crouched like a frightened
dove, passing my nights
on the edge of my bed.

Never had anyone felt so ugly.

I hardly recall the remainder
of the story; it dragged
past like a sluggish drug.
No one in the country used the
word 'civil' anymore.
In the aftermath of theft and war
came more war, more blood
and sudden changes.

My sister had murdered her
child-killing husband on his return.
No woman blamed her, none
except her daughter Elektra.
And that was the one who mattered.
Elecktra goaded her brother
'til he broke with rage and slaughtered
his own mother.

And me. I was not only a slave,
I was a murdered slave, by my own
sister's children. The old maternal
order flooded in blood the day
the two conspirators climbed
the steps to my jail tower.
It was my worst hour, and I hardly
remember it. They have said that
I did not die normally, but flew
into the heavens and became a star.
Venus? was it? Beauty.

I have been trying for centuries
to recall exactly why
I left my original queendom,
was it on such shaky ground?
Downward bound?
Why was I dragged back
into such a state—
Do I lie sleeping?
Will I wake?

A Queen am I. Queen Helen
and a Sovereign.
Flama. Shaker alike of earth
and of the heavens.
a queen am I
Queen Helen is my title.
As the sun shines so shines Helen

most beautiful, most blamed.
I am what ever is,
the weaving tree
and Mother of my people.
and I shall be
the Mother of my people.

Paris and Helen

He called her: golden dawn
She called him: the wind whistles

He called her: heart of the sky
She called him: message bringer

He called her: mother of pearl
          barley woman, rice provider,
          millet basket, corn maid,
          flax princess, all-maker, weef

She called him: fawn, roebuck,
          stag, courage, thunderman,
          all-in-green, mountain strider
          keeper of forests, my-love-rides

He called her: the tree is
She called him: bird dancing

He called her: who stands,
          has stood, will always stand
She called him: arriver

He called her: the heart and the womb
          are similar
She called him: arrow in my heart.

One for Helen

What did the Greeks steal
when they stole Helen of Troy—
what was the loot, the beauty?
Was it only a face, some graces—
a sex toy?

Doesn't even she remember how she spun
twine from her woolly distaff, and strung
cords in a line with even spaces
on a wooden frame? And as she wove
the songs she sung were played upon
another kind of loom which has become
the fundamental harp. The music staff
unraveled from the weaver's staff,
the notes taken from the knots,
the shuttle reshaped into a bow,
the resinated strings—
all these were her things.

This was viola
da gamba, violin, cello,
the chamber with strings, the singing in
and of, the loom. From her room,
the wooden belly of her
chamber, came the sitar, twelve string
guitar, piano, banjo, Kyoto,
clavichord and zither. The electric bass.
This (and not her face)
was the original, the real lute. The instruments

of Helen, when she was a poet,
a singer and weaver.
She emitted so much music! in her work.
They heard. They pried open the door.
And these are only some of the things
they took her for.

Helen's lover

When he was a young man he had skin
that glowed like pollen, and
with his swollen blossom lips,
his afternoons of energy, his hips,
his dense leaf smell—
with such a spell around him of vitality
and certainty, how could I ever
say I'd never love him, who was like
Paris, in the springtime,
ship in my harbor, sun in my windowsill.
When first he arrived, the swell
of birdwings beating all around him,
there was a flutesong in his eyes;
'forever,' he whispered but even as
he spoke the pollen blew
forever off his lips, the ship grew
cannon, and then conquerous. Now the grown
man lunges up my steps, so armed, so
dangerous, drunk with a different
determination. Did he kill
the young man, simply, his body
left for dead beside me in
my house of smells, my beaten
birdwing feelings, my own body
beginning to weigh me down,
and for a mate, the heavy
hated one, the one who's treated me
a captive, the one I've treated
as a foe?

Old Helen

Discarded in old town, bunched,
wearing indigo blue
worsted leg veins,
you were a beauty once,
Helen, weren't you—
before the ships came.

You were a beauty once
before the ships came
to your (uh-oh) rescue,
bearing gifts or promises or chains,
field labor or the mills,
warping you with pain,
debts or deadly chemicals,
spinning your beauty down
to an empty spool in old town.

You were a beauty once
Helen, a singer and a weaver,
spinner and a storyteller too,
of greatest fame,
before the ships came.

Now your face shows
what you have had to know
about the use of beauty,
youth, flying fingers too
(where they fly to).
You know the first name of the booty

they got, and as you lug
your burdens down the street
with no one to help you,
you remember what they mean by "rescue."
You were a beauty once
Helen and you will be.
Your expressions prophesize.
The anger migrates through your veins
like great flocks of flesh-devouring
birds, wheeling and diving, gathering the drives
to unknit the terrible patterns of our lives.

In the tower of the crone

The small town streets were neat
and orderly the day I met the hag.
She was trying to catch a cab
to the downtown drugstore, illicitly
to fill her morphine habit when
she spotted me.

The hag smiled, blue eyes bleary.
What a disheveled, needled thing
she was, coat worn
over a pink slip, hair rank,
a nest of unremembered chores.
I pitied her, stared at her gold teeth.
I was sixteen
and avid for adventure.

She held my unassuming face.
"What beautiful expressive eyes
you have," she said. "You ought
to be a star, an actress."
I was bedazzled. "I was an
actress once," she said. She laid
her hand upon my arm.

And I became apprenticed, following
her home. Not to a tower, exactly,
though a jail: a square hole
with unmade bed, crawling with cats

and flies and maggots, open cans of
catfood stinking everywhere.

My whole heart bled.
Still, I stayed. I put her to bed.
"I played with Ethel Barrymore,"
she said, "and dear John, on the stage
and in the movies."

My mother punished me when I got home.
Forbade me to return to the old crone.
But I was in a trance, nevertheless,
a success-trance. I too would tell
tales on the American loom.

A month later I read of the once-known
actress found dead, after three days,
in her room. And I learned:
          the price of first is last
          the price of fire is ash,
and don't go into the weaving room
alone, alone
don't go into the weaving room
alone.

Helen in Hollywood

When she goes to Hollywood
she is an angel.

She writes in red red lipstick
on the window of her body,
long for me, oh need me!
Parts her lips like a lotus.

Opening night she stands, poised
on her carpet, luminescent,
young men humming
all around her. She is flying.
Her high heels are wands, her
furs electric. Her bracelets
flashing. How completely
dazzling her complexion,
how vibrant her hair and eyes,
how brilliant the glow that spreads
four full feet around her.

She is totally self conscious
self contained
self centered,
caught in the blazing central eye
of our attention.

We infuse her.
Fans, we wave at her
like handmaids, unabashedly,

we crowd on tiptoe pressed together
just to feel the fission of the star
that lives on earth,

the bright, the angel sun
the luminescent glow of someone
other than we.
Look! Look! She is different.
Medium for all our energy
as we pour it through her.
Vessel of light.
Her flesh is like flax,
a living fiber.
She is the symbol of our dreams and fears
and bloody visions, all
our metaphors for living in America.

Harlowe, Holiday, Monroe

Helen
when she goes to Hollywood
she is the fire for all purposes.

Her flesh is like dark wax, a candle.
She is from any place or class.
"That's the one," we say in instant recognition,
because our breath is taken by her beauty,
or what we call her beauty.

She is glowing from every pore.
we adore her. we imitate and rob her
adulate   envy
admire   neglect
scorn   leave alone
invade, fill
ourselves with her.
we love her, we say

and if she isn't careful
we may even kill her.
Opening night
she lands on her carpet,
long fingered hands
like divining rods
bobbing and drawing the strands
of our attention,
as limousine drivers in blue jackets
stand on the hoods of their cars
to see the angel, talking

Davis, Dietrich, Wood
Tyson, Taylor, Gabor
Helen, when she goes to Hollywood
to be a walking star,
to be an actor

She is far more than a product
of Max Factor,

Max Factor didn't make her
though the make-up helps us
see what we would like
to take her for

her flesh is like glass,
a chandelier
a mirror

Harlowe, Holiday, Monroe
Helen
when she went to Hollywood
to be an angel

And it is she and not we
who is different

She who marries the crown prince
who leads the processional dance,
she who sweeps eternally
down the steps
in her long round gown.
A leaping, laughing leading lady,
she is our flower.
It is she who lies strangled
in the bell tower;
she who is monumentally drunk and suicidal
or locked waiting in the hightower,
she who lies sweating with the vicious jungle fever,

who leaps from her blue window
when he will, if he will, leave her

it is she and not we
who is the lotus

It is she with the lilies in her hair
and a keyboard beside her,
the dark flesh glowing.

She whose wet lips nearly swallow
the microphone, whose whiskey voice
is precise and sultry and overwhelming,
she who is princess and harlequin,
athlete and moll and whore and lady,
goddess of the silver screen
the only original American queen

and Helen
when she was an angel
when she went to Hollywood

The Inheritance

How we have each labored
to create this civilization,
most of us against our will,
without our knowledge, thrilled,
enthralled, appalled or stalled
in this industrial serfdom
known as 'modern man';
this card game with its temporary flush,
founded on the village skills of
ancient women and their men, distilled
drop by drop from all the liquors
of our many lives, that electrifying
amber glow, that aura of what
our bodies do and know,
that history we can tell and show,
so trivially classified as 'work'
and 'workers.'

Trivially classified, enlisted,
tagged—
brought from an old
Old Country
in small sacks,
the scientific-magic of our
former ages,
bagged like the wind
and sold, breath by breath,
solo by solo, riff by riff
and measure after measure, as if

it were all free, and not
accumulated treasures
of complex creatures
such as you, me. The wind.
A tree.

The grandfather wind, the
mother tree, the message
delivered like genes, like
green beans, or
language given to a child,
accumulated patterns to be
used or listened to, as recipes
or tools or principles,
the message
passed along a long wind, the
whistling of a dancing bird
upon a dancing tree: Nothing is free,
everything belongs to one another,
nothing begins new, everything has
a mother, a father, and a story.

Frigga with Wuotan

The physical principle
of energy is this: the flame
lives inside the wood
as the erotic charge
lives in my belly. He
comes in to get it
with his beautiful
magician's stick—the one
that is his own. He
says that I enflame him.
I say that we enflame
ourselves.
Rubbing the sky's electric wand
like this, in the groove
of the earth's soft woody substance,
to conjure some creative fire
is an old human trick;
tribe upon tribe
has arisen from it.

Frigga with Hela

Her fingers
within me
    a spindle
my feelings
    woolly
her dear hand
    axis
on which my internal world
    whirls.

"She is making me"
on the whorl of her love
turning me out and in
transforming patterns.

So I say of her,
"she is making me,"
    and I mean she is
making me over,
again.

The Queen of Wands

And I am the Queen of Wands.
Okay.
Here is how the world works:

It is all like nets.
ever golden, evergreen
the fruits fall
into   hands-like-nets
the fish are hauled
into   jaws-like-nets
the insects crawl
into   claws-like-nets

and the thoughts fall
into   minds-like-nets.
it is all like nets.

On the other hand
a spider lives in the topmost branches of a pine,
her house a god's eye gleaming among the needles.
On hot days
she pays out her line and
twirls on down
to the surface of the lake or pond
to get a little drink of water
and to wash her face. She's such an
ordinary person.

The trees line the earth, great and small,
dogwood, plane, maple, rubber,
the elegant palm. The scrubby oak. The elm.
We're ordinary persons, too. We have our
long time friends across the distances,
our urgent messages and our differences.

And we have our parties.
We sugar up our petals just to get the probes of bees in us.
Most green ladies love everything the whipping wind can
          give them.
The avocado tree hung with her long green breasts,
she aches for fingers pulling at her;
the cherry, peach and nut trees bent with swollen balls
long for hands and mouths and claws;
the fig tree with her black jewels tucked between her
hand-shaped emerald leaves, is happily
fondled by the dancing birds, wild and raucous and drunk on
natural fig wine.

almost any summer morning
sun beams fall into my arms like lovers
giving me everything they've got
and they're so hot   oh honey
I take it all

give it to me, baby
is my song

And I am the Queen of Wands.
The people honor me.
I am the torch they hold over their own heads
as they march march like insects
by the billions
into the bloody modern world,
over discarded corpses of their ages past,
always holding me, aloft or in their arms,
a flame in the hand of the statue,
a bundle of coals
in their inflammatory doctrines, calling me
a chalice of fire,
essential light,
the Flama
and the stuff of which their new world will be made.

Sophia (Helen) they call me, enlightenment,
"God's light," wisdom, romance, beauty, being saved,
"Freedom," and the age of reason.
Progress, they call me, industrial revolution,
"People's rule," the future, the age of
electronics, of Aquarius, of the common man and woman,
evolution
solar energy and self reliance. Sexual self-expression.
Atomic fission, they call me, physics, relativity,
the laser computations in an endless sky of mind,
"science," they call me and also emotion, the aura of
telepathy and social responsibility, they call me
consciousness, "health," and love

they call me, bloom of Helen.
Blush upon her face, and grace.

And here I am a simple golden shower.
and here I am only a spider
webbing their minds
with pictures, words, impulses
feelings translated into moral imperatives
and rules for living, like leaves
upon a tree, spread to catch the sun's attention.

They (the billions of people)
dance like Fairies on my smallest
twiggiest branches
whistling in each other's ears,
collecting and dispersing
seeds, wearing gold and
pretty clothing, worrying and not
really noticing all the other worlds
around them
how the sun center of my eye sews them
how the silver dream filaments direct them,

how their own thoughts connect them, how
the baton smacks their knees to make them
move their feet, that baton
at the end of the claw
of the Queen of Wands

And I am the tree
with candles
in its fingers
the tree with lights
Menorah
Yule-flame
tree of life

the tree-shaped
candle-holder
on the mantle
on the altar
on the flag of being.

And I am the Queen of Wands
who never went away
where would I go?

the flame is central
to any civilization
any household

any bag of bones. Any motley mote
you've got, of
little mustard seed can grow
into a yellow spicy flame
as you must know.

The sun is a weaver
and the rock earth her instrument.
Slender-fingered threads of light
and heat, dance like birds
shuttling.
Winds and the rain,
seeds and feet and feathers
knit the knot
making the great coat,
the coat of all colors.

The coat of all colors;
over the whole earth, a caught fire
of living logs, brown and red,
tan and white, black and yellow
bobbing like a forest;
each a magic stick with
green flame at its tip

a green web
my leaves, my green filaments
like fingers spread
to catch the sun's attention, spread
to catch the sun like thread,
like sexual feelings, like
the gleam from an eye, or an idea.

and I am the Queen of Wands
I am who stands

who always will
and I am who remembers
the connections woven, little eggs
along the message line.

I remember giving dinosaurs
to the tall unfolded ferns to entertain them
and immortality to the cockroach.

I remember the birthday of the first
flower, and the death of so many furry
animals and kinds of people, and a star
that fell. I remember a continent
of green
green wands of grass
burning into the knees of
buffalo queens, a landlocked
ocean of fire. Replaced by the
picket fence. Almost equally complex.
Sky scrapers like spikes.
But that's another song.
And I am the Queen of Wands
who burns, who glows, who webs
the message strands,
who stands, who always will.

The good weef is both

The good weef is both
weaver and wife, those old
words meant the woman-as-a-maker,
not especially bonded
to one husband,
but to the Spider Woman of life,
the one with ties that bind,
knitter of the sacred, magic knots,
who with her scissors or her knife,
is tie-breaking life-taker,
queen of what-is-not.

Wife and weef and weaver,
she was the market-woman
of Europe. Ale-wife, she sold
the ale she brewed; oysterwife bawled
what from the mothersea she drew,
strawberrywife what she grew.

The fishwife brought her stinking
reputation with her to the modern ear,
reference, they say, to a certain smell,
said with a certain sneer. The smell is
of queens.

The midwife stands midway
between the laboring weaver and her weaving
and the world, easing the way to life.
I am pleased to call myself a wife too,
a word-wyfe.

But I mean any kind of thief

When I went
looking for the Foe
I called him "he"
the one in the fast
car and the outside lane,
the getaway man
who came and took
and went, a stranger

but I mean any kind of thief—
of souls, pride, the heart,
of land, space, air and work.
I mean the thief of truth
of meaning

the one who goes
by what is said
and not by what is done
that one
that kind of liar
the fantasizer

smoker of bad wishes;
the cold one who, shivering
steals your thunder and your fire
then calls you poor,
calls you "Queen of Wants"

and wants.

When I went looking
for the Foe I thought of
boots and leather, barbed
wire fences, aggressive
legal stances and the
colonizer
who takes the heart
out of your sky, diverts
the light from your eye
into his own

but I mean any
kind of Foe, her, the
sap-sucking cannibalizer,
idea-eater, and the one,
the ones who make war
with rents and wages

the masked mate,
who makes war with love
and personal rages
the raper who takes
your sense of self
and wholeness,
flame of trust
and leaves you trembling,
crusted with his fear.

the daisy bringer
who calls you Queen for a day
and takes your year

the friend who cries on your shoulder
and never sees your grief
who looks in your mirror
and calls you low
and calls you less
than who you are
I mean the Foe
that one
I mean any kind of thief.

Knit the knot:
a riddle

The directions said:
to knit the knot known and
not to knit the not known,
knit the knot known
to the unknown knot
and not the knot known to
unknot the unknown
and knot the knit;
to unknot the known and knit
the unknown, unknit the
knot known and know the knit;
to know how to not know
the unknown, knit the knot.
Gnaw your fingers to the bone
until you understand the plot.
or not.

Spider Webster's declaration:
He is singing the end of the world again

He is singing the end
of the world again,
he has sung it before.

When he flattened Troy to the ground, seven times,
left Carthage salted like a fat old hog,
Africa, "conquered," he said, he announces,
he is singing the end of the world again,
millions burned in Europe, butchered in
Africa, millions blown to bits in China,
Russia and now in Central and South America,
thousands of tribes
and villages destroyed, the matrix
of whole peoples, cultures, languages, genetic
pools, ways of describing, gone, gone,
apparently, according to his song, whirled up into
his description of the past.

He is singing the end of the world again,
he has sung it before.
Americans fly over their world and its ghosts,
Americans stare at their own ghosts without
recognition. Invisible the Indian ancestors,
invisible the Mayan-centered
feather industries, invisible the
great buffalo and the buffalo queens,
old ladies of the hip high buffalo grass,
invisible the engineering systems, amphitheaters,
philosophical wholeness in the old

civilizations of the mind.
Occasional sulky sacred bears
stare from the cages of zoos
refusing to acknowledge men as their children.

He dwells in threats of fire, Armageddon, Hiroshima, Saigon,
and Tyre, Berlin, Gomorrah, Hell itself,
the story of fire, his theft of it. "Put
a huge wad of flame on
the wand's tip. Wave it,
shouting: Fire, Fire."

The whites of their eyes stare
back at him.
There was a city *here*, once, once
there was a city (and now there
is another)

There was a tribe
and now there is another,
there was a nation here once
and now there is another.

He is singing the end of the world again.
He has his song
and I have a long, long
wand like memory.
I remember five worlds
and four have ended.

I see (I can't help it)
buffalo faces in the gloomy white
people of Iowa, waiting slump shouldered
for the light to change,
chanting, "We used to rumble the earth here,
once, with the charge of our electrifying
hooves. Now in the midst of the stolen
golden corn
standing in their fields like sacred groves
surrounded by plenty we are oddly depressed."

He is singing the end of the world, again.
Reincarnated bears
prance and sway in the lowlife bars of
this place calling itself a nation; they
lean, pissing, on the wall in Dallas,
Detroit, Charleston, Denver, hold intellectual
discussings in great roars,
knife each other, make predictions.
They await the Bear god, the Bear Maiden. They
are not concerned with the form this will take,
it is their form, they will take it.

Dancing birds leap out of the young faces
kissing on the streets of San Francisco, Salt
Lake City, Memphis, leaping with an urgent
sky-message; and the lovers call what they
are feeling, "love," "desire," "relationship."
They do not know to call it,

"Birds dancing."
Birds *do* dance, and so do
ghosts, and buffalo.
Spirits line shoulder to
shoulder on the highways shouting
Maya Azteca Aztlan Olympus
Mississippi Valley Seneca Falls Cibola
Shangri-La, The River Niger, Hollywood,
Tibet. Atlantis. Eden.

There was a nation here, once
and now, there is another.
Business people pat each other's pinstripes,
putting their own names on the ancient remedies and
products, systems and understandings. "Let's
design a rocket out of here. Don't forget to
bring the queen of buffaloes. It gives me such
satisfaction knowing she is mine. Let's pretend
that we are doing this for sex,
for money."

He is singing the end of the world again
he has done it before.
He has his firebrand
and his song.
I have a long, long
wand like memory.
I remember five full worlds
and four of them have ended.

Helen your beauty:
a chorus

Helen your beauty—
is it a meteorite? or
is it as cold, and
is it as tight, and
is it as gold
    as gold?

Some things are dry goods
some are wet
some are to covet
some to get.

Helen your beauty—
is it your blush,
is it innocence?
what is untouched—
or is it what touches?

Helen your beauty—
is it what gives, or
what is blamed,
is it what lives, or
what is enflamed—
or what flames?

Helen your beauty—
is it emotional?
a hot-flush
or a rush?

Is it a halo or a psychic glow,
Helen your beauty—
is it your soul?

Helen your beauty—
is it as light, and
is it as bold, and
is it as bright, and
is it as old
    as gold?

Like a woman in childbirth wailing

A queen am I
my city is within me

ever and ever did I swell
with its messages
delivering all it ever needed
to know of itself
cell by fleshy cell
and spark by spark
and all entirely in the dark.

I plied on the smallest, starkest loom
inside the smallest, darkest room
knitting fingernail to finger
iris to eyeball to socket
I rarely missed a stitch.
Almost the hardest thing I had to know
was when to call the baby done
and let it go

nor did I have to lug the burden
by myself

     I, when the wind spirit
     swole me up
     sisters surrounded
     to hold me up.
     Ours was the whole birth,

and the power of blood
and the bread and roses.

Ours the riddle of the ring
releasing even as it encloses.

Ours the molecules of flesh
on the helix spindle
ours the spinning of the whole earth
with its knots and bundles.

Ours the word
when the word was spoken,
ours the zodiacal belt,
the axis moon, the time of month,
the herb tea taken.

Ours the babe
when the womb was open,
ours the singing, the chants,
the counting string,
the new fate woven;
ours the circle that remained
unbroken.

And then one day the Foe came.
He with his forceps.

he with his forceps
to replace my muscles, his
pincers, metal instruments
instead of grandmother's long fingers
and my midwife, whom he killed.
Who he destroyed in such tremendous
numbers. Tied and tried. Condemned.
She stood high in the flames
like the Queen of Wands
her faggots blazing all around her.
How we wailed when she was burning,
hiding, running, our child's eyes
from the fleshfire turning.
He called her a witch,
he with his mask and swords.
But I did not stop him

He was so clumsy then
He tied me up and
turned me upside down
to birth against the force of gravity,

sewing me back together like a doll
because I ripped, I tore, my organs
dripped down my legs in my old age.
And if they spoke of this at all,
the mothers to the daughters
spoke with rolling eyes, in horror;

and when I complained
he drugged me for the pain
so then my babies choked at birth
of overdosed brains,

        Oh how long, how long before you
        must our hearts be cast in pain,
        o queen of heaven, queen of the dark chamber,
        Lilana, queen of sheep-folds, Nana queen of childbirth
        holy woman, child begetting . . .

a queen am I
my city is within me

ever and ever did I swell
with its messages. And now
he is passing me by.
like a man
in a myth
I now give birth
through my side, my belly,
gut sliced open to accommodate
his glove—while I lie passed
by, unconscious, thieved
of all my beauty—my volition.

No wonder they call it
Caesar's operation.

Still, it saves lives.
That is the hook
he has me on.

This industrialization
of love, of birth,

this is the last besieged castle
the last tower
and of this particular war
this is the last hour.

the great, pink walls
of this genetic treasure cave
are being shaken
and this will be the final city
ever taken.

Blow, whistling wind, blow
the filament of
breath that stirs the feather
from within the egg, the cave,
the place of birth, the city

built of flesh, the muscular
enclosure, bag of skin
that holds us in and gives us rest
and motion, meaning and sweet
method. Oh womb, cell spinster,

as you know
the only real production *is* love.
I mean the ties between all unlike beings,
minute connections on
the message line, the one continuous knotty cord

(oh spider Webster) wrapping us together,
I mean that esthetic, feeling-chested
glow, electric field of quickening,
the envelope of thought
and feeling dropped
over the still flesh
like a golden, animating net.

a queen am I
my city is within me

it seems that
he and I are joined
to make another
kind of being

and what I call "make"
he calls genetic engineering.

He reproduces flesh, metallic
organs, miles of pumping blood
in plastic veins, hormones in

powder form; he transposes parts,
his a factory womb, producing
factory beings, healed and cut
with laser beams; someday
I will have removable
dayglow-colored viscera
in soft purselike plastic.
I can give my heart away
quite literally.

> The cow wailed
> and in her place lay down.
> Like a woman in childbirth wailing,
> she wailed, the cow wailed
> and in her place she lay down.

May there be a breast
to nurse my child
and may there be
a chest to hold my heart
and ears to cup my words,
and may there be a bird
to dance my story.

Beauty, sleeping
(Who shall wake us?)

Who shall wake us
if we don't ourselves
shake loose the sleep
of ages, animate the doll
at last and bid her
rise, and move and rule.

Who will wake us from our
dream of capture
if we don't ourselves
shake loose the long spell,
the illusion of being small
and silenced, sourceless
and unheated.

Who will be all knowing
and the prince if *we* don't
make him happen, somehow
groom him for his task
to rouse us from the suicidal
slumber.

(And the Foe if no one else
knows how to shine his boots
knows how to stride
to the tower steps
and rocket up to shake us
from our sleepy lives

with fear. But I don't mean
the Foe, I mean another
and ourselves)

Let the prince come
integrated and sure
let it be time
for a man strong in his
insides
without boots or
a broken brain, let him
have a golden net
around him

Let him arrive now
in any form, as a Bear God
or computer programmer
or even a dyke in a man's costume
let his step resonate the steps
of the hightower

Mothers mothers raise him
tell him, make him
who will wake us
who will wake us
who will wake us from our
trance of ages
if we don't

Ourselves prepare
for that reception;
animate the doll's flesh
for the kiss of life
of recognition,
animate the doll's will at last
and bid her rise
and move and rule.

Grand Grand Mother is returning

The egg is always being made
and making,
always getting laid
and laying;
thread is being spun
and spinning,
truth is being found
and finding,
getting all unwound
and winding,
being all unsnarled
and snarling,
and the Grand Grand
Mother is returning

that's all I know

Don't suppose it will be
as it is remembered
in time past

time present is a different
unpredicted
picture

time future happens
only in the mind

Worlds are always ending
and beginning,
tales are getting learned
and learning,

birds are always taking off
and landing;
the sky is ever being turned
around, and turning;
the tree is ever being stood upon
and standing;
and the flame is getting burned
and burning

Grand Mother is returning
don't expect
the past, expect
whatever happens,
men are moving, more
than ever women are
just wakening;
"Grand Grand Mother
is returning

that's all I know"*

*quoted from words spoken by Paula Gunn Allen

selections from

The Queen of Swords

(1986–1987)

In *The Queen of Swords* we discover that Helen's story goes back much further in historic time than Troy, at 1200 bce, to a time a thousand years earlier when she was a goddess in ancient Mesopotamia (present-day Iraq). But my story brings her completely up to date as a middleclass privileged woman who leaves her husband and embarks on an adventure in an "Underworld" lesbian bar. The story that is told is that of the goddess (Inanna, Venus) who descends to the underworld and goes through transformations. Her older sister, Queen of the Underworld, has her killed and hangs her on a peg for three days and three nights. She is brought back to life by androgynous beings made by the god of sweet waters. But prior to this various warriors from different eras tell how they resisted oppression, trying to get Helen, who has lost her memory of her own power, to be less passive. The play here is also on the cultural splitting of the category woman into sexually, racially, and economically defined tokens of good and bad, above and below, and the objectification of some women/people as "light" and some as "dark."

The story is also that of a privileged woman coming to terms with her own shortcomings, taking responsibility for her own participation in oppression of others, and finding comradeship as a woman among women.

Students and young people, in my experience, love to perform scenes from *The Queen of Swords*. They tell me they appreciate its sexual and political daring, its biting wit, its verbal lushness, and the rare opportunity "to chew" a woman of privilege "down to something honest" in the characters of the Crow Dikes, whose job it is to turn conventional meaning on its head. The excerpts don't begin to do justice to the many themes in this postmodern drama, so I just chose a number of poems because I like them for themselves.

The signature poem of the Queen of the Underworld is "Descent to the Butch of the Realm," and this retells the ancient story in sexual terms. It is an amazing, quickening experience to read this poem for an audience. My favorite lines in this epic however, are these: Everyone wants Love to be his own/ to be her own/ everyone wants Love to follow them down their road/ But what is it Love wants?/ where is it Love wants to go?

Everyone wants Love to be his own

Everyone wants Love to be his own,
to be her own.
But what is it that Love wants,
what does Love want to know?
Everyone wants Love to follow them
down their road;
where is it that Love wants to go?

It isn't easy being Nothing

It isn't easy being Nothing
it isn't simple being down
but someone has to do it—
for the sky to turn around.

We can't all be in our places
in an orderly form;
someone has to be chaotic
for the sky to turn around.

The wind is Nothing's true lover;
where the wind lives
is Nothing's true home,
out on some street corner picking up crumbs;
high on some mountain, down in the dumps.

What Nothing does is hold the place
completely still, for Zero.

It isn't pleasant being no one,
the eye in the eye of the storm;
but someone has to make the spaces—
or the sky would never turn around.

Nature doesn't give a damn

Nature doesn't give a damn
if I'm not or if I am.
All the sounds of life I hear
sound the same without my ear.

Yet stars affect me just the same
as if I were affecting them;
and I love no less the sea
for its never loving me.

Butterflies and birch trees
are unaware of pleasing me.
Earth needs no love to give.
We love. What other cause to live?

Crow chorus with Helen

Crow	Who's unnatural?
Crow	Nature.
Crow	Well, that's only natural.
Crows	She's finally getting some sense.
Crow	What could be more unnatural than nature?
Crow	Always interfering with the course of my life.
Crow	Always changing everything, ever notice that?
Helen	Men are so violent.
	Woman is more like Nature.
Crows	Women are not violent
Crow	And I am not violent
Crow	And the Queen of Swords is not violent
Crow	And violence is violet
Crow	And Americans are not violet
Crow	And the wind is never violent
Crow	And the sea, the sea is not violent
Crow	And nonviolence is not violent
Crow	Nonviolence is inviolate
Crow	And the earth is not violent
Crow	And a shooting star is not violent
Crow	And a volcano is not violent
Crow	And war is not violent
Crow	And violet is not violent
Crow	And nice is not violent
Crow	And nice is not viola
Crow	And men are not violent
Crow	And mice are never violent

Crow	And the deer are not violent
Crow	Except in the woods
Crows	Where they live
Crow	But in the movies they are not violent
Crow	And the woods are not violent
Crow	And puking is not violent
Crow	And death is not violent
Crow	And cars are not violent
Crow	And Americans are violas
Crow	And violas are sometimes violent

The sky is a sheet of crystal on a day like this

The sky is a sheet of crystal
on a day like this.
A person could easily fall through
into an abyss.
You could find your astrological aspects
reversed,
your path crossed, your luck
cursed—
on a crystalline day under a crystalline sun
you could fall from this
familiar life
into some other one.
You could come untied,
open one door and enter another one.
You could begin this day
with a solid position in your class,
a marriage built on tradition,
an education, a vocation and an aim,
and having no further explanation
than that you fell through a sky of glass
on a particular crystalline day like this—
have none.

There is more to standing

There is more to standing
than simply having standing, and more
to understanding than simply falling down;

there is standing your own ground.

Amazon Chorus
(As for what we do with horses)

As for what we do with horses
it's none of your business,
it's none of your knowing
what rides we mounted
what circles rode, what songs shouted.

It's not for your understanding
what fires we kindled
in autumn darkness,
what flames we handled
when the moon was
breathless.
                    As for what
we did in tandem
it was the bonding of warriors,
as for what we did of ritual.
it was what you now call: actual.

As for what we learned in shadows
it's not of your fathom,
it's deep as molasses
or a parade of motorcycles,

As for what we do with horses
we ride them like forces,
as for what we do with forces,
we tug them in closer.
As for what we do with borders
we cross and uncross them,

as for what we do with curses,
we put them in purses
and fling them to blazes.

As for what we do with horses
we fondle their noses
we drape them in roses
and race them on courses,
it's a greathearted outpouring
with the whole crowd cheering,
it's not for the artless,
it's how their hoofbeats whisper up
to us, "Destiny, destiny, destiny . . .
rides on solidarity."

It's the brave heart churning,
to nearly bursting,
it's the pent blood pressing
the hot breath
to the hotter neck,
it's the hand slapping and the wet flank
slapping back against the hand.

As for what we do with horses,
it's the rush of our great trying,
it's the tension of our lunging
it's the love of promising
it's the flesh imagining itself flying
it's the flash of light before thundering,

it's the dark ring of opening,
it's the way we have of living
in the dust of the wind.

I, Boudica

I, Boudica,

a queen am I,
a warrior and a shaman.
Shameless is my goddess and ferocious;
my god's foot cloven.

I am protectress of my horse-bound clansmen.
A red-haired, full-robed, bronze-belted swordswoman.
I am a queen of sacred groves and other old realms
where astronomers divine from droves of animals
or flocks of birds, and study the signs in palms:
a queen of times when men are lovers to the men
and the women to the women,
as is our honored pagan custom.
Ever and ever did we think to reign
in such an independent fashion,
until the day the foe came.

He came to my temple.
In ships he came to me.
Our possessions upon the prow of his ship he put.
He with hired soldiers came
to our self-ruled regions.
The foe, he with legions, entered my court.
He put his hands upon me, he filled me with fear.
My garments he tore away, and sent them to his wife.
The foe stripped off my jewels and put them on his son.
He seized my people's lands and gave them to his men.

He put his hands upon me, he filled me with rage.
I spoke to him in anger.
I told him of his danger.
So for me myself did he seek in the shrines.
In front of my folk he had me beat;
and this was not the worst I had to meet:
he seized my young daughters and had them raped.

He seized my daughters
and had them raped;
oh queen of heaven, queen
who shatters the mountains;
how long before you must my
face be cast in hate?

A queen am I, my cities have betrayed me.
A queen, Boudica am I, my cities have betrayed me.
In that rebellious year
of sixty-one A.D. I rose up,
I, Boudica, over the countryside
from clan to clan and ear to ear,
I drove round in a chariot,
my daughters with me.

To every woman and every man
I spoke:
        "Now is the battle drawn
        which must be victory or death.
        For today I am more than your queen,

and more than your mother deeply wronged,
I am all the power of women brought down;
one who will fight to reclaim her place.
This is my resolve. Resolve is what I own.
We women shall fight. The men can live,
if they like, and be slaves.

And so we went to war.
Our men went with us.
And for centuries since, the foe has
searched for us in all our havens,
secret circles, rings and covens;
almost always we elude him,
we who remember who we are;
we who are never not at war.

On that day
didn't I, Boudica,
didn't I up rise,
didn't I slay,
didn't I hold fast
the ancient ways.

Wasn't I like a wall
wasn't I a great dike
against a giant spill,
that iron sea
of Roman pikes
that came to conquer Gaul.

Even if for one day
didn't the foe almost fall,
didn't his teeth gnash,
wasn't his bladder galled,
didn't the foe, even he,
know fear;
he feared me.

He feared me, then,
in his being
unable to fully win
unable to fully kill
the rebel things
my name means,
he fears still.

He fears me still,
for my shameless guise
and lesbian ways;
for undefeated eyes,
a warrior's spine
and all my memories
of women's time.

A queen am I, my city
needs to find me.
Meantime the foe arrives
unceasingly
from every steel-grey sea,

by every mountain road on earth
he enters all my cities
and for me myself he seeks
in my varied shrines,
in my temples he pursues me,
in my halls he terrifies me,
saying, "Cause her to go forth."
He goads. He burns, he murders.
He erodes.

A queen am I,
a warrior and a shaman.
Shameless is my goddess and ferocious,
my god's foot cloven.

A queen am I, a living memory
who knows her own worth
and who remembers that the future
is the past rehearsed.

      and *not should I go forth*
      unless it be for battle girthed.
      Unless it be for battle girthed,
      and belted, *not should I go forth*

      until the foe is driven from the earth.

I am Ildreth remembering

All in green I rode a tall horse
deep in the North woods, my hair
so yellow it was white and fine and
down to here.

Big as any conquering Viking man I tracked them
and by trickery caught one or maybe two.
Stepping noiseless behind I ran
one fellow through
before his ax could pop my skull.
Blood along my scabbard told the others
to steer clear.

Protecting other women and the children
and the older people was my task.
Proof is here on my face, in this new mark . . .
I studied in the mirror this morning
getting ready for work . . .
or was this from just last weekend
when I, racing nowhere in my car,
wrecked it, going head first
through the windshield and being
drunk when the cops came,
got out, of course, and blindly fought them
and was beat raw to the pulp
that left, from cheek to jaw,
this deep pink scar?

I swear I'm going to quit this life
of drinking whiskey, trying to keep
a girlfriend—spending all my money
in the bar.

I'm going up to the country to build a house
with my own hands,
find some ground—to love,
to leap, and land upon.

I'm going to the country to build a house,
maybe invite a few friends,
some strangers—people in my same bind,
no name for what they're doing in
their sacks of skin.
Going to go looking for my real mind,
the one I think I once had
before my memory got lost.
Going to sit at the back of my house
and gather my old thoughts
          like scattered birds,
and make images of mud,
and words and glass,
and gather my old gods
          like a flock of birds
from a soulplace,
and touch my fingers
gently to my own
and to my lover's face,
and study up.

Her shadow falls across me

I don't know my motive or my gain,
I know her shadow falls across me
where I lay.

I know we must have been close
since now she's gone
I walk my life a ghost.

I don't know our middle or our end.
I know in our beginning
we were friends.

I don't understand her motive or her gain,
I don't know where she's been
or where she'll be again.

I know my life is not the same
without her flamboyance, or her flame,
I know her shadow falls across me where I lay.

I know I must be feeling bad
since now when I sleep
it's underneath my bed.

I never undertook to know her mind,
I'll never know her motive
or her plan.

I know her shadow falls across me
where I stand—

A woman among motorcycles

I remember a time, a night when the sky
was a sheet of crystal, and the air was dry
I became a Woman in the Middle of Motorcycles.

One night, a night of the full moon
rising just as Venus lowered in the West,
I went out walking, miles
into the hills, alone,
not even my dog went with me.
It never occurred to me to carry a gun.
I crossed an abandoned parking lot
whose asphalt had begun to rot,
with grass and thistles already pushing
thinly through,
and the first roar of the motorcycle
only startled me,
then two more, then three,
I wasn't frightened until they were five
and circling me, their black boots
and jackets armor against the moonlight.
Dense with terror, I turned to see
they were ten, all single men, grinning
and grim and watching me.

I knew instinctively this was not the time to fall.
Begging, showing fear or pain would be my death.
I drew a great first breath
and throwing back my head, I called down the moon,
"Mother Moon," then

"Mother Venus," I called,
as the cycles crawled past, circling and waiting,
and roaring and watching me.
And then I said my mother's name
and hers and hers and hers and hers

Grandmother Mabel I said,
Grandmother Kate I said,
Grandmother Clementine I said,
Grandmother Mary I said,
then I called my aunts to me,
Margaret, who baked bread when grandpa died,
Helen I know nothing of at all,
Agnes spanked me till I cried, Sybil helped build her
own cinderblock house by the shores of Lake Michigan,
Gertrude who wasn't mechanical drove her
very first car straight up a telephone pole.
Betty worked forty years in a grocery store,
and Blanche wore a high-topped dress,
black stockings, a brilliant smile
in the only photo I have seen,
when she was seventeen, in 1917.

When I had finished with my aunts,
I called the gods and mothers of the gods, Mary,
Anna, Isis, Ishtar, Artemis, Aphrodite, Hecate, Oya, Demeter,
Freya, Kali, Kwan Yin, Pele, Yemanya, Maya, Diana, Hera, Oshun,
and after that some saints, Barbara, Joan, and Brigit;

as my memory ran out I made up some more saints,
canonized them on the spot.
And finally I called my friends including from high school,
then each woman I have ever worked with,
then some heroines, till I had chanted every woman's name I knew.

When I was through I said them all over again,
turning in my own circle with my face up and the moon
shining in, it must have been an hour or more I whirled
and chanted, filling my ears with my womannaming roar.

When I opened my eyes
the angry men were gone;
Venus had set, the moon was down,
I stood in the asphalt field
alone—
and not at all alone.

Descent to the Butch of the Realm

I am your wild cherry sister, red and
black sheep sister of the unkempt realm.
I am the Butch of Darkness and the Lady
of the Great Below.
I have a nickname: see if you can guess it.
Thistles in my fur are twisted
taut as wily wires of gristle.
You won't find me sitting home in front of TV
drinking beer, not me—I'm outdoors
prowling midnight. Nor do I march
to take back the night with other women
for I never lost it.
My name is Shadow of the Wolf,
I woof and I whistle.
My usual companionlover's name is "Destiny."
She had it tattooed
on my upper arm. She is, of course,
a Dike. She chews me down to something honest
on a weekly basis when I let her.
Oh! But I have plenty of time for you
and your bright beauty—
yes, I have plenty of room for a Venustype
such as yourself
in my chamber.
Remember me now whenever
you hear the phrase "wild cherry."

Oh descend
Descend to me

to my exhilarating gaze
and my desiring
Yes it is true—I am who wants you
and I hear you have chosen
to come down to me.

Strange to everyone but me that
you would leave the great green rangy
heaven of the american dream,
your husband and your beloved children,
the convenient machines,
the lucky lawn and the possible
picture window—to come down here below.
You left your ladyhood, your queenship, risking
everything, even a custody suit,
even your sanity, even your life.
It is this that tells me you have a warrior
living inside you. It is for this
I could adore you.

Now I want you to enter my stormy regions.
My gatekeeper will guide you; where
do you think you
want to go? Just ask his howling
hollow center.
His name is "Nothingness."
I want you to stand as I stand before you,
tremulous with expectation
as I reach to tangle all my fingers in your hair

to rip away the veil of your
perpetual smile, and then to strip
off your scarf of limitations, even
the birthright of your long hair itself.
Do my stark eyes surprise?
My name is "Naked of Expectations."

And I want to bend you
as I am bent to nip your neck, unclasping
your lapis blue necklace. Ever notice how it
keeps you from talking? You are going to do
a lot of talking. And no small amount of yowling.
Are you certain you should have come?
I may never release you.

Oh descend
Oh lower yourself to love
in the underground, the union
of a woman to one other
woman, not self to self
but self to other
self.

Slap your feet flat on the earth now,
heel first preferably, thrust
your pelvis forward.
You see I am about to change
your center of gravity.

As for those explanatory notes and diagrams
tucked under your arm—put them down.
You won't need them.
You will be too busy with your own internal
computations, as I lick between
your fingers, slipping off the golden rings
of definition and adherence.

Oh descend to me
lower yourself into yourself
as I go down
and go down
and go down to you.

I want you to fall, as I fall
heavy lying next to you, your twin egg stones
happy underneath my hands, the
pearl-pearl buttons I'm unsnapping,
then that thickribbed brassiere that gives you
all the cleavage you have used to
get your men to hope and grope
bearing gifts and favors.
You are your own gift now,
and you have chosen to come to me.

I of the snarled hair, the one earring
and the brassy metallic nailpolish,
I am your wild cherry sister. I am savage,
living in regions ruled by laws

that to you just happen.
When you say "just happen"
you will remember me.

I want you to crawl
unravelling
as I crawl over your dancing belly
to unbuckle the belt of willingness,
last obstacle before you splay your doorway
to my doorway. Reveal to me.
You have a secret self, don't you?

Can you bear your heart to be split
open and to lie so naked
in the sight of
either one of us?

Oh descend to me
mound on mound of Venus meeting
maddened Earth to be unbound on.
Fix your gaze upon me
while I find and flay you
with my fingers and my tongue.

My tongue is nicknamed
"Say Everything."
She's appealing enough
at first until she nails you fast

to solid dirt of the fat earth
and ends your fantasy.

You will moan, Inanna
you will cry.
Everyone you ever were
will die,
while you go down
and go down
and go down
on me.

Hanging helpless on a peg of feeling
as I bear you to your
new and aweful place of being, locked in
dead heat, we will argue. We will
fight. Your heart will ooze like red meat.
I will suffer too, to birth you,
to transform and finally release you.
I am cruel, yes. Exacting and not
possibly fooled.
Pain opener. You want pity for your
little yellow egg of being
broken on my greasy griddle.

I am pitiless. And stirring
I will sear you, so when
next you say "you puking, putrid

lying selfconceited wretch you"
it is my face you will see,
my name you screech out "Oh! I'll Kill!
That Rotten! Bitch!"

Yes, I am the Butch of the Realm, the Lady
of the Great Below. It is hard for me
to let you go.
When next you say "you bitch"—"wild cherry"—
and "it just happens"—

you will think of me
as she who bore you to your new and lawful
place of rising,
took the time and effort
just to get you there
so you could moan Inanna
you could cry
and everyone you ever were
could die.

Ever wish upon a star?

Imagine if you couldn't call it by its name.
Imagine if you only knew how far away it is,
and its specific gravity,
what would you wish for?

Is a plant a what?
Is a ghost a who?
Imagine thinking that a made-up television character
is a real person but your dog is not.

Is a street who if it has a name
And what if it has a number?

Measuring the mettle of a person
or measuring the person of a metal
or meddling in the meter of a motor
or metaling the measure of a mother,
would you lose some of the stars you see
if you could count them only by their names?
Is counting a way of praying?

Thoughts are points of sound/light

Thoughts are points of sound/light
sheathing
stratospheres.
From up there
I have watched human beings
thinking they think.
Really, they hear.
Tuned in to radio bands
of collective understandings,
flashes of insight
going inside from outside.
Once in a while
a group magnetizes
a thought form, called
"a new idea," a sound mote—
and blaring it out
gets it caught up there in the sheath
where it's available
to anyone else who wishes to share,
and to think they thought
by shifting their inner ears.
Interesting idea, this
that I thought I heard
while I was there.

the mother of trees is dirt

the mother of feel good is hurt
the mother of all is none
the mother of found is gone
the mother of talk is breath
the mother of laughing is death
the mother of beauty is memory

I fell through a hole/
in the eye of death

I fell through a hole
in the eye of death;
I drew Zero's breath.
I went to where the wind lives—
I put my ear there.
I went down below.

The eye is a sheet of crystal
on the other side of time;
the sky is a paradigm.
I could see myself reflected
in my inner and my outer mind.

Deep in the eye of death
the light is never standing,
it's dancing, it's unfolding,

light is holding dark,
shy is holding bold,
hot shelters cold
in the partnership we have
with death that is not, is
not dying, is glowing,
is chancing.

I'm no longer lying
in my cave of glass, I'm rocking,
I'm shaking,
I'm expanding

I went all the way to Zero,
leaned in Zero's door;
and you know what lives in there?
Absolutely everything-everything at all.

We'll laugh it off to burrow /
in a lighter cloth of time

As hour by hour, I go on growing older
I like the carrion crow
as my advisor.
Not many are more wicked, not many are wiser.

For adviser I'll take the carrion crow
to stand upon my shoulder
with his caw-caw coffin chatter
keeping me self conscious.

Keeping me so super conscious
that my flesh, however pretty
and however dear to me
belongs to someone else tomorrow
(or to no one)
and is only borrowed clay.

Is only modeled clay, my loves,
to animate the fray
and we'll slough it off to burrow
in a lighter cloth of sky.

In a lighter coat of sky, my bird,
to lay out the next play,
we'll cough it off to burrow
in the beauty of the sky.

As for beauty of the being,
it isn't fixed in time
longer than the ching ching ching
of a wind chime.

It's an animating play, my crow,
of light on surfaces.
Like the carrion bird I carry
on my shoulder, beauty strips away
the dross so we can fly—

in a lighter coat of sky, my friend
in a wind chime's clime—
and we'll laugh it off to burrow
in a lighter cloth of time.

The Ice Queen

She lives on a glass mountain
She sleeps in a fishbowl
She's wrapped in Saran Wrap
She's silent under her bell jar.
She's locked in her tower of glass.

She's Queen of the Ice Queens.
She feels none of her feelings.
She acts none of her actions.
She speaks none of her insights.
She hears only the crash
of her own cold pulse
and the words: it's getting worse
and worse
and worse.

Is this what dying is really like?

I have the sensation of needing to regulate
my every breath;
of my life being something I stand and watch,
a falling star against a falling sky—
reality I thought I had in hand
suddenly dropping down
a funnel of air—

I have the sensation
of the black hole of creation
squeezing me through its bloody gate
to what's out there—
what's out there?

I wait. I cannot breathe. I shake.
What if I admit, admit, admit,
and still can't make sense
of any of it?
What if I'm crazy?
What if I never again act right?

What if everything—
even the mirror of sound and sight—
is a lie?
What if all I ever do is die?

What if I don't, and hate every minute
of staying alive?
Is this what being born is like?

Dancing in Place

Oh Lady, Lady of the changing shapes
help me remember
how to dance in place;
when to witness,
when to harness,
when to charge with all my forces.

I don't know the reaches of my fate.
I know your shadow falls across my face.

Oh Lady, Lady of the Great Below.
Hard are your lessons,
many-fanged your harshness;
irresistible are your passions
and sweet, sweet are your praises.

I don't know the mazes of your soul.
I know your shadow falls beside me
everywhere I go.

New and Future Poems

(1987–2006)

Even when I'm not conscious of the role of spirituality, it permeates my world and saturates my poetry with language of communion and mythologies of nature and collectivity. As I work, nonhuman beings crowd in, demanding voice and contributing power. Spirits stand tall along the wall in my late night room, suggesting ideas, beaming energy, answering pleas, making jokes. Or that's one way to look at the process of listening to the air, or waking up with lines in mind. On the other hand trained poets will recognize "Forest, forest" as a hand me down from William Blake's "The Tyger."

This section includes "gift poems" that stem from my sense of wanting to offer something directly to one other person. So, "The Mother of All Bowls" was written on the occasion of an honoring for Luisah Teish. "Talkers in a Dream Doorway" is meant as a tribute to the erotic as a force between artists, following a dinner party with a small number of lesbian writers in 1986. The flirtation is an infusion of energy fueling the desire for change, as Audre Lorde was first to acknowledge. Belly dancers express love and spiritual community this way as well. Some of these poems carry the element of desire as a spiritual and transformational force, into a variety of metaphors—a diversity of bowls, or a family of whales adopting the spirit of the late poet philosopher Gloria Anzaldua, whose deity of choice was Yemanja, the great Ocean Mother of Yoruba tradition. The "gift" in "Gratitude to you for the food of our abundance" is for MamaCoatl, who with her own passionate arts, forced my attention onto immigrant workers from Mexico hearing terrible things about themselves on every side.

Three of these poems are stanzas from longer work; I hope the greater meaning can shine through—the butterfly in the excerpt from *Mental* for instance is meant to evoke a particular quality of joy I have experienced at times in the company of persons with schizophrenia. "The Vampires of Empire" is also from a longer poem, *women are tired of the ways men bleed*, a call for changes of ritual in these fear-driven war times. The poem is sound-based and I perform it with musician singer Anne Carol. Red Hen Press plans to publish a collection of my "nine part" poems, including "A Woman Is Talking to Death."

"News," on the other hand is the only poem I saved in a series of "little thoughts" sent with the rent check every month to my landlady in Oakland, in the superstitious hope the (mostly cheery) words would prevent her from evicting us. The ending poem, "may we embrace" is an invocation to my inner sense of "all peoples" written for the conference "Body and Soul" sponsored in 2004 by the Women's Spirituality Program which I co-direct. Is poetry the intersection of natural and human forces, in verbal form. . . ? If so, this is yet another course of commonality, stretching wide.

The Vampires of Empire
from "women are tired of the ways men bleed"

just as,
—as the Kogi have told us
gold is the blood of the Earth—
oil is the blood of the Mother

the Mother's rule
is blood for blood
you eat, you pay

we drink her blood
to fuel our lives
our rule is *glug glug glug*
we're free, we say

if we can't have more than our
more-than-our-share
we call it a crisis
and go to war

we pay the price
an addict pays
if oil costs the blood
of 4,000 soldiers
we don't care
if it costs the blood
of 600,000 civilians
we don't care
if it costs the blood
of 30,00 traffic deaths
we don't care

we are the vampires of empire
we can eat cherries in winter
we can fly anywhere
everything we do begins with petroleum
yum yum yum

what did we do this year?
we drank, drank
the blood of the Mother
burp burp burp
we burned, burned
the blood of the Mother
rumrumrum
we drove round
in carriages,
as fast and as far as we could
slurp slurp slurp

sweet syrup, so
free—we are free
we live in a sea
of burning blood

we can drive anywhere
don't need roads
the earth is our road
our rule is *lug lug lug*

we love our carriages
roomy, safe, we carry homes
and offices with us
pretend our trailer
is a wickiup
make a procession of carry-out,
pick-up
go go drink drink burn burn

where are we going?
what is the purpose of the trip?
we don't care
we love the sensation of getting there
salty illusion of being free
we are the vampires of empire

we go wherever our addiction takes us

the Mother doesn't care either
doesn't intercede
You Eat You Pay she says
and all natural history confirms
she means it.

Gratitude to you for the food of our abundance

Campesinas y campesinos
gratitude to you gratitude to you
and to your ancestors
gratitude to you for the food of our flesh and bones
the nourishment, the steaming sustaining good nourishment
the sun and moon fine food that feeds me and feeds so much of the world

gratitude to you for maiz, maiz, maiz
red-yellow-blue-white corn smelling of morning noon and night,
mother of so much humanity
gratitude to you for red and green chiles, for bright pink pinto beans,
for the redbrown elixir of the heart, chocol'ate, chocol'ate, xocoatl
gratitude, gratitude, food bearing basket of hundreds of millions

los indigenas de las Americas
gratitude, gratitude to you for the food of our abundance
north American abundance stands on the wisdom of the ancestors
of indigenas, their co-creation with the spirits of potatoes and peanuts,
of tapioca roots and tomatoes, of white beans and squashes, of cranberries and
strawberries, and the spirits of wind and the mountains, and sweet rain.

shame shame to the American corporate growers
who use NAFTA as their weapon, who use NAFTA to undermine
you farmers and drive you from your land
who use subsidies to undersell you, who drive you out of business,
who drive you to come north for cash, for cash, that inedible drug cash
to subsidize your farms so you can keep them

shame shame that Americans don't know this, don't recognize
the problem of immigration begins at home in the US nation,
in accumulations grown not from co-creation with spirit
but stolen with money and legal manipulation,
those cold old gold oppressors of the earth
to drive the mother people out of business is surely a grave grief sin
earth does not forgive all the sins we visit upon her
until we change our behavior, and then she devours them like compost

let us begin to say welcome, welcome, welcome
to your country, welcome again to the land of your ancestors
may you acquire your share of the abundance, the abundance, abundance
you have already provided to so many
may the earth be with you
may the people of all lands be with the earth
and be with you

Forest, forest

Forest, forest burning brown
at the fulcrum of our flight.
Forest rabbit, human hound,
caught in 'all we love is light'.

All we love is burning down,
Nagasaki's eye is bright.
Human hound without an ark,
air, water, earth, and dark.

If we wish upon a star
wish upon a fish instead.
Wish upon a sapling's girth
wish upon a mossy glen.

Wish upon an earth's delight,
wish upon a change of worth.
In this moment of resound,
take a black and forest heart.

Take our dark and forest heart
hurl it at our light struck mind.
Planets fall so deadly still.
Unless—exertion of our will

in a love with forest joined,
at this burning turning point,
on this whirling churning dot.
Do we have a will, or not?

think what a butterfly
from "Mental"

think what a butterfly does to our life
that's elemental

there is nothing substantial about a butterfly
it doesn't feed you or give you a bed
it doesn't remember what street we live on or how old you are
There is nothing about a butterfly we would want to take to
the insurance adjustor, nothing incremental.
But think what a butterfly gives us
of delight, think what surprise in that flutter of life
and how amazing the colors, who would ever have imagined
such combinations as a butterfly takes for granted
in its short display of light play
and that sacramental face, those sensitive antennae
connecting to our inner eyes.

There are dances, notions and inspirations
we can't know except for butterflies
that we can't know when there are no butterflies
when life is detrimental
and when the habitat, the habitat of butterflies
is so destroyed
what is the covenant
we must have with butterflies.

Talkers in a Dream Doorway

You leaned your body in the doorway
(it was a dim NY hall)
I was leaving as usual—on my way.
You had your head cocked to the side
in your most intelligent manner
eyes glistening   with provocation,
gaze direct as always,
and more, as though wanting something,
as though I could have bent and kissed you
like a lover
and nothing social would have changed,
no one minded, no one bothered.
I can't testify to your intention.

I can only admit to my temptation.

Your intensity dazed me, so matter of fact
as though I could have leaned my denser body into yours,
in that moment while the cab waited
traffic roaring nine flights down
as well as in my ears,
both of us with lovers of our own
and living on each end of a large continent.
We were raised in vastly different places,
yet speak this uncanny similar tongue.
Some times we're different races,
certainly we're different classes,
yet our common bonds and common graces,

common wounds and destinations
keep us closer than some married folks.

I admit I have wanted to touch your face, intimately.

Supposing that I were to do this awful
act, this breach of all our lovers' promises—in reality—
this tiny, cosmic infidelity: I believe our lips would first be
tentative, then hardened in a rush of feeling, unity
such as we thought could render up the constellations AND our
daily lives, justice, equality AND freedom,
give us worldly definition
AND the bread of belonging. In the eye of my imagination
I see my fingers curled round the back of your head
as though it were your breast
and I were pulling it to me.
As though your head were your breast
and I were pulling it to me.

I admit, I have wanted to possess your mind.

I leaned forward to say good-bye,
aware of your knuckle possibly digging a tunnel
through my thigh, of the whole shape of your body as
an opening, a doorway to the heart.
Both of us with other lives to lead
still sure why we need so much to join,
and do join with our eyes on every
socially possible occasion.

More than friends, even girl friends,
more than comrades, surely,
more than workers with the same bent,
and more than fellow magicians
exchanging recipes for a modern brand of golden spit.

I admit we have already joined more than physically.

The cab's horn roars.
You smile, or part your lips as if to welcome how I'd just
slip in there, our tongues nodding together,
talking inside each other's mouth for a change
as our upper bodies talked that night we danced together.
Your face was wine-flushed, and foolish; my desire selfish,
pushing you beyond your strength.
You paid for it later, in pain, you said.
I forget you are older, and fragile. I forget your arthritis.
I paid later in guilt, though not very much.
I loved holding you so close, your ear pressed to my ear.
I wanted to kiss you then but I didn't dare
lest I spoil the real bonding we were doing there.

I admit I have wanted to possess my own life.

Our desire is that we want to talk of really important things,
and words come so slowly, eons of movement
squirt them against our gums. Maybe once in ten years a sentence
actually flashed out, altering everything in its path.
Flexing our tongues into each other's dreams, we want to

suck a new language, strike a thought into being, out of the old
fleshpot. That rotten old body of our long submersion. We sense
the new idea can be a dance of all kinds of women,
one we seek with despair and desire
and exaltation; are willing to pay for
with all-consuming passion, AND those tiny boring paper cuts.
I never did lean down to you that day.
I said good-bye with longing and some confusion.

I admit to wanting a sword AND a vision.

I doubt I will ever kiss you in that manner.
I doubt I will ever stop following you around, wanting to.
This is our love, this stuff
pouring out of us, and if this mutual desire is
some peculiar ether-marriage
among queens, made of the longing of women
to really love each other, made of dreams
and needs larger than all of us,
we may not know what to do
with it yet but at least
we've got it,
we're in the doorway.
We've got it right here, between us,

(admit it) on the tip of our tongues.

Margedda's Hair
from *Mundane's World*

Margedda's hair is the crest of a male bird at the height of the mating season, the season of show-off. Things do not go into her hair so much as they appear constantly to be popping out of it—long rods of metal, huge wooden or tortoise shell combs, intricate gold panoramas suspended on stilts walk about easily in Margedda's hair, which is also like the sea in a beautiful storm; Margedda's dangerous hair. It rises and foams and ebbs, forms caves, plains, peaks and tendrils that drip down her neck and the fronts of her ears like simple vines.

In its many forms it changes by the hour, extending herself so far in any direction that to imagine Margedda without her hair is like imagining someone else without a face. Margedda's hair is horns and antlers, manes, crest and peacock tail, elephant ears, and cities seen from a great distance. Nothing extraneous to her comes near it, out of respect; it is not meant for touching, it is for the eyes to see what they dare; the hands could learn nothing from it.

Margedda's hair speaks of what is possible, and what is not. She makes of it an organic sculpture, careful as if it were granite and could only be done once, temporary as a one day moth. Nothing can change Margedda's hair, change is its only name, incorporating wind and straw, dust and rain into its body, giving them meanings they would never think of themselves, without Margedda . . . Margedda can be very simple when it is a simple day, but looking into Margedda's hair especially if any one is concentrating, is to see the many wonders of your own mind and the transformations of your life. Since this can be dangerous, everyone uses Margedda's hair with precision and thoughtfulness.

Inside Passage

listen my younger
friend, the fifties are a broken
step, you wake to realize
your thirty-five year old self
has died and no one in the town
bothered to tell you. Her certain
cinch is winning, her method:
running.
After awhile she yowls an invitation
through your window and in rage
you imagine thoroughly
burning down the house.
What keeps
you cool is not now
the question where
your life is going but rather
what, and whom
you love.
Unclench to answer this and sixty year
old self glides toward you, hand
outstretched, warm and
gladly grabbing on,
you're wearing rose
and turquoise once again
on center stage, feet planted and
committed.

Goddess of wind

days of joy
days of brood
days of grief
days of rage
you sweep in
on the wind
as if you were real
send me reeling
weeping wailing
I find a cause
I find a story
to match the mood
I find a blame or credit
to suit the feeling

Kira and Pete in the ninth month

Swim out little fish
restless as electric eel
you kick and thrash
pirouette or shimmy
in your mother's silky
sterling pool

swim fast little fish
be outward bound
toward acoustic steel
reverb of your father's sounds

into welcome wide spread hands
the nets awaiting—you. Who binds
with one that tightly sweetly holds,
and one that swings and lets you go

News

"All the news is bad,"
say the ants.
"We slip and slosh
as we carry our young
to higher ground."

"All the news is good,"
say the snails.
"We slide and glide
on greener blades
and shells grow round and round."

"All the news is old,"
says the rain.
"The air decides,
the sun colludes,
the earth absorbs
and I am all that's ever new,
—and only while I'm falling down—
as soon as I hit ground,
I'm used."

Mothers, fathers, clasp the children
from "women are tired of the ways men bleed"

Mothers, fathers, clasp the children, tie them to your breast and beam
like flashlights, hold the children praise them with buckets
of raspberries, shiny as jelly, give them you.
Show them they are green-worthy as grass in rain, lofty
as kite-flying by the Bay, sharp as sunrise after an ice-storm.
Grasp them, study their eyes, talk to them like kittens.
Tell them they have the sturdy grace of deer, communal peace
of stones, generosity of the sea, able, able, capable and ready.
Tell them they can learn to be happy no matter what else is true.
Mothers fathers grip the children with bearpaws of glee,
press them to your hearts, sing high into their precious ears,
drip strawberry down through their lives, tell the sons they are ships
and shores, tell the daughters they are mountains and towns that will
thrive a hundred years, say the world is sending them a ticket,
they just need to find the train that's theirs.

Oh winds of change, gather the wounded
boys and girls of all rages
into your giant arms, blow brotherly breath
across their fierce sad eyes, unclench their wish
for motherly porridge, pour fatherly tears
of crooning through their bliss-hungry lips
and tell them this:
when we find or make that motherplace
our vessels heal, contain no leaks
and all around us love pours in, red cells pulse
and burn away bleakness
red cells flash as curious pretty fishes
spelling the words
"this is my darling life, and this is enough"

Gloria, daughter of Yemanya

as the mother rocks you gently
you will remain heard
as seaweed knocking against the dock piling
insistent, dedicated words,
breaking barriers, mixing currents
you will remain respected

people will hear your name
as an aim
written in waves
they themselves ride
shouting, "sea change, sea change"

you are in good company
following the dark whales
on their way to warmer water
where they bear their young
and glide north in a pod to be
sizeable moms with boisterous children
together again, in the soft bays of California
spouting the froth of her swells

we hear your voice
in the low tone of the sea bells
in the optimistic squeal of gulls
you are never alone.

for Gloria Anzaldua
2004

when you walk down this road

when you walk down this road
winding through your favorite grove of California
old live oaks, venerable sharp bark smelling
place holding, smoldering old live oaks,
you won't notice at first
the skin of their trunks as twisting tawny torsos
of slow slow dancers
rippling their hips across the centuries
of knowing each other, feeling secure in the strong winds
between them, roots tangled underground in constant
communication.
you'll notice, instead, or one of you will,
the hard round leaves, ecstatically green
shiny, small and licentious,
shivering in the air as you are unaccountably shivering,
pressing hands, excited, looking for a space to be
together, both of you with quivering eyes on the nipples
hung over your heads in acorn shapes, the air between you
stung alive with light as though centuries ago
you set up this union of enchantment that you pray
that you pray
will stay with you
everywhere you go.

October 20, 2005

On the happy occasion of the wedding
of Jaime Jenett and Laura Fitch
and, as ever, for Kris

lunarchy

go with the tide, with the moon,
where despair
never lasts
always returns to joy
and joy
never lasts
returns as fear, and

fear is
fleeting with birds in the wind,
ebbing mad, then
flooding joy, beautiful, dreadful and
steady as the morning star
that rises, falls,
fills, empties, fills,
disappoints, fulfills
drowns, buoys,

and disappears
reappears
the way she does
the way love does,
steady, unsteady, steady
unsteady, steady

may we embrace

Great Mother, Great Spirit, Great Mother-Father God
may we embrace
those whose deity is a talkative stone,
a sacred tree or a reindeer
may we embrace
those whose deity is a complex historic story
of martyrdom, suffering and redemption
may we embrace
those whose deity is immanent in a dance of joy,
in drum-song, or a literate tattoo carved in flesh
of sacred human body
knowing yours is the greatest of all bodies

Great Spirit, Great Father-Mother God, Great Mother
may we embrace
those whose deity is the keeping of just law
and may we embrace
those whose deity is the breaking of unjust law
may we embrace
those whose deity is a sexual being, and
those whose deity is a breath of sound, and
those whose deity is crafting a talisman of jewels
or a beautiful cloth, a painting in sand
of our lives as paintings in the wind
knowing yours is the gift of thoughtful action

Great Father-Mother God, Great Spirit, Great Dancing Mother
may we embrace
those whose deity drips gore

in the eternal bone yard
of the nonreality of any body
and may we embrace just sitting with all being
and may we embrace
those whose deity is present in a tender kiss
of the baby god
and the blessing of all relationships
knowing you are the blood red web holding our short lives
on this long earth

Great Mother, Great Spirit, Great Father-Mother God
may we embrace
our own hearts
may our hearts stretch large
as wombs
as consciousness
as the river of life
you of the nebulae and the black holes
you of the microbes and spinning cells
you of the shimmering cosmic delight
may our hearts stretch toward your heart
you of the largest heart

may we embrace

Biographical Note

Judy Grahn teaches and co-directs the Women's Spirituality Master's Program at the Institute of Transpersonal Psychology, where she is Associate Core faculty. She also teaches in the Interdisciplinary Arts MFA at the California Institute of Integral Studies in San Francisco. Her email is jgrahn@itp.edu. Along with Deborah Grenn, she writes for and edits *Metaformia: A Journal of Menstruation and Culture*, at www.metaformia.org. She considers this new origin story the most important (and the most fulfilling) work she has yet done, and a growing number of people are in agreement. She earned her Ph.D. in Integral Studies from California Institute of Integral Studies.

Judy has published an earlier poetry collection, *The Work of a Common Woman*, and two book length poems, *The Queen of Wands* and *The Queen of Swords*. Both have been produced as plays; Wands toured Europe and England in 1986. She has also published four books of nonfiction, including *Another Mother Tongue: Gay Words, Gay Worlds*, and *Blood, Bread, and Roses: How Menstruation Created the World*. Her novel is *Mundane's World*, an ecotopia; she has also published essays and short fiction.

Judy is working on a history of Gay Women's Liberation, and "The Queen of Cups," as well as number of other projects. She appears in the Canadian film, *Stolen Moments*. She has given about a thousand readings and presentations.

Some of the poems in this collection are excerpts from her new nine part poems, "women are tired of the ways men bleed," about changing our rituals; and "Mental," about the category of "crazy." These are available on her home page, www.judygrahn.org. She performs with musician/singer Anne Carol Mitchell, and recently opened for Ani DiFranco's West Coast tour.